Light Therapeutics

A Practical Manual of Phototherapy for the
Student and the Practitioner

_____

By JOHN HARVEY KELLOGG, M.D.

Author of "Rational Hydrotherapy," "The Art of Massage," etc., Fellow
of the British Royal Society of Medicine, Fellow of the American
College of Surgeons, Member of the American and British
Associations for the Advancement of Science, the
Société d'Hygiène of France, American Society of
Microscopists, American Medical Association,
Medical Director of the Battle
Creek Sanitarium

THE MODERN MEDICINE PUB. CO.

BATTLE CREEK, MICH.

Copyright 1910 and 1927

Kessinger Publishing's Rare Reprints
Thousands of Scarce and Hard-to-Find Books!

We kindly invite you to view our extensive catalog list at:
http://www.kessinger.net

Preface

The first edition of this work, published seventeen years ago (1910), was one of the first extended treatises on the therapeutics of light, and the writer believes was the first dealing with the use of the incandescent light bath and the first work of any sort undertaking to correlate the use of the light bath with other forms of physiotherapy. Since its publication, numerous books on the various phases of light therapy have appeared, several exhaustive treatises; but none, so far as the writer's knowledge goes, have emphasized the important point of combination and correlation of light applications with hydrotherapy, electricity, thermotherapy, diet and other appropriate measures.

The greatest handicap to the progress of physiotherapy has been an inveterate tendency to exploit each newly discovered agent or method as a panacea, or at least to make use of the new agent by itself alone instead of associating with it one or more appropriate measures. As a result, failure has often resulted when success might have been attained by a more rational procedure. Monotherapy may be sometimes needful as a means of demonstrating the value or efficiency of a new remedy, and sometimes a single agent or method may meet all therapeutic indications; but a carefully adjusted combination of physical agents will often attain brilliant results, when any one of the several measures employed, if used alone, would accomplish nothing.

The writer's experience in light therapy, extending over more than 50 years (1876-1927), has convinced him that of the many physical agents which lend themselves to therapeutics, light is one of the most potent, although for obvious reasons, less versatile and less available than some other agents. As a prophylactic measure, light has no rival except fresh air, and fresh air and light are usually associated. The lack of sunshine is probably the dominant factor in cloudy regions in raising the death rate from tuberculosis and degenerative disorders through prevention of normal development and the lowering of vital resistance.

With these general considerations, however, this book does not undertake to deal; the purpose being to present in a concise way the fundamental facts of light physics together with a brief description of light appliances and the technic of their application and a summary of the progress in clinical light therapy which has been made in recent years, since the first edition was published.

In the present edition, a number of chapters have been very largely rewritten and very extensive additions have been made. Credit is given in the text to authors from whom quotations are made; but special mention should be made of the excellent works of Rollier, Leonard Hill, Bernhard, Saidman, Mayer, and especially of the highly valuable papers of Sonne, of the Finsen Institute of Copenhagen, Denmark.

The writer desires especially to express his appreciation of the advantages for original research afforded by the well-equipped physics laboratory of Battle Creek College, the special investigations conducted by the able physicist in charge, Dr. W. J. Hooper, and the interesting papers prepared by the research fellows under his supervision. It is, in fact, only by close connection with a physics laboratory that it is possible to check up old methods and technic or to develop new ones.

In the first edition of this work, the writer expressed the opinion that the time would "soon arrive when no hospital will be considered completely equipped which does not include in its outfit a full set of electric light appliances for therapeutic use." That day has dawned and the interest in light therapy and light as a prophylactic agent has risen to such a high pitch of fervor that the day cannot be far distant when every college and every public school, will be supplied with facilities for sun baths, and artificial sunlight supplied by arc lamps will be installed in schools, factories, office buildings, college dormitories, nurseries, and in well furnished hotels and private homes. A large part of the civilized world is living in the shadow and becoming wan and weazened in consequence. The time has fully come when the whole population should be stirred up to follow the injunction of Holy Writ to "Walk in the light."

JOHN HARVEY KELLOGG.

Battle Creek, Mich., Jan., 1928.

Preface to First Edition (1910)

This work does not profess to be an exhaustive treatise on the subject of either light or light therapy. It is intended, rather, to serve as a practical manual for the clinical use of the electric-light bath in its various forms, and in its various applications, general and local.

An effort has also been made, in a small way, to correlate the light bath to those other forms of rational physiotherapy which naturally and profitably associate themselves with this newest of physical curative measures.

Twenty years ago this work could not have been written. The electric-light bath had not yet been devised. The photophore, and most of the other therapeutic methods and appliances described in this manual were not even dreamed of. Probably no non-medicinal remedy has ever found its way so rapidly into general favor as have devices for utilizing the physical properties of light in combating the inroads of disease.

The first incandescent light bath was constructed by the author in 1891. After it had been used in the treatment of some thousands of patients at the Battle Creek Sanitarium, a bath was exhibited at the Chicago Exposition in 1893. Mr. Gebhardt, a visitor from Germany, saw the bath, visited Battle Creek to become familiar with the technique of its use, and on returning to Germany began, with the "Sanitas" Co. of Berlin, its manufacture and sale in that country. German medical men and financiers soon recognized the value of the method. Winternitz of Vienna constructed a bath after the author's description, which was first published in a paper delivered by request before the American Electro-Therapeutic Association at its fourth annual meeting, held in New York, Sept. 25, 1894.

The bath soon became highly popular in Germany. Hundreds of Light Institutes were opened in the leading cities. King Edward of England was cured of a distressing gout at Hamburg by means of a series of light baths. He had the bath installed at Windsor and Buckingham palaces. Emperor William soon after followed his example, as did King Oscar of Sweden and several other of the crowned heads and titled families of Europe.

In time the fame of the bath spread back to its home. The Kny-Scheerer Company of New York imported a bath from Berlin as a therapeutic novelty. The last few years have witnessed a growing interest in phototherapy and the time will soon arrive when no hospital will be considered completely equipped which does not include in its outfit a full set of electric light appliances for therapeutic use.

Trusting that this volume, incomplete and imperfect as it is, may prove of practical use to some of those who have recognized the value of this new method in the clinical management of many forms of chronic disease, the author submits this little work to his colleagues in the profession, craving their consideration and criticism.

J. H. K.

Battle Creek, Mich., 1910.

CONTENTS

Preface   3

Historical   9

The Physics of Light 11

The Physiologic Effects of Light 23

Light Therapy 68

The Technique of Light Applications 89

The Arc Light 103

The Incandescent Light Bath 116

The Quartz Light 131

Thermotherapy 135

Clinical Phototherapy 151

ILLUSTRATIONS

Spectrograms 10
Diagrams Showing Range and Penetrating Power of Rays.. 14
The Original Carbon-Arc Therapeutic Lamp (Kellogg) 20
Effects of Heat upon the Skin.......................... 72
Diagram Showing Relation of Superficial to Deep Circulation 84
Diagram Showing Relation of Superficial to Deep Circulation
    —Posterior 85
Cutaneous Reflex Areas (Anterior)...................... 86
Cutaneous Reflex Areas (Posterior)..................... 87
Battery of Sun-Arc Therapeutic Lamps.................. 90
A Sunshine Playground................................. 92
A Sunshine Playground................................. 93
Outdoor Gymnasium of the Battle Creek Sanitarium....... 96
Sun Bath Combined with Sand Bath..................... 97
The Solar Arc Lamp.................................... 103
Twin Arc Lamps with Reflector Housing................. 104
Arc-Light Bath with Two Arc Lamps.................... 106
The First Arc-Light Cabinet Bath (1897)............... 106
Arc Light to the Spine................................. 107
Arc Light to the Spine in Reclining Position............ 107
Arc Light to the Chest—Over Stomach.................. 108
Arc Light to the Abdominal Region...................... 109
Application in Reclining Position....................... 109
Arc Light to the Scalp................................. 110
Arc Light to the Face.................................. 110
The Photophore (Kellogg).............................. 125
A Portable Folding Electric Light Bath................. 127
Application of Photophore to Upper Spine............... 128
Hydrotherapeutic or Douche Apparatus.................. 138
Douche Apparatus, Showing Control..................... 139
The Wet Sheet Rub.................................... 145
The Cabinet Air Bath.................................. 148
The Abdominal Heating Compress....................... 149
Sun and Open-Air Treatment of Tuberculosis............ 180
Tuberculosis of the Spine (Rollier)..................... 188
Tuberculosis of Spine and All Large Joints (Rollier)..... 188
Application of Arc Light to Ear—To Abdomen............ 193
Case of Leucoderma Three Weeks after Beginning Treatment 198
Dispersion of Light Rays by a Prism.................... 198
Leucodermia Showing Return of Pigment................. 198
Case of Leucoderma Six Weeks after Beginning Treatment 199
Case of Leucoderma Treated by Arc Light............... 200
The Arc Light with Cooling Fan (1910)................. 208

LIGHT THERAPEUTICS

Historical

From the earliest ages, the sun was worshiped as the source of life and creative energy. The most ancient monuments of the remote past are the ruins of temples dedicated to the worship of the sun.

The predecessor of Tut-ankh-amen, Aknaton, initiated the worship of Ra, the sun god and composed hymns in his praise. Recent explorations have brought to light many tablets extolling not only the sun itself but the power of which it was held to be the symbol, and sculptured representations of the royal family enjoying a sun bath while doing homage to the King of Day. Here are a few lines from one of the poems of this famous and highly enlightened monarch whose concept of Deity may have been in some respects more lofty than that of the ancient Hebrews:

> "Thy dawning is beautiful in the horizon of heaven,
> O living Aton, Beginning of life!
> When thou risest in the eastern horizon of heaven,
> Thou fillest every land with Thy beauty;
> For Thou art beautiful, great, glittering, high over the earth;
> Thy rays, they encompass the lands, even all Thou hast made."

Hippocrates employed and extolled sun baths and heat for the treatments of wounds and fractures.

Herodotus attributed the thick skulls of the Egyptians to the fact that they shaved their heads and were much in the sun.

Pliny, who lost his life at the eruption of Vesuvius which destroyed Pompeii, habitually took a sun bath daily in summer before lunch, and it was just after he had taken such a bath that he was summoned to the rescue of the victims of the great disaster in which noble effort as director of the Roman navy, he died, smothered by the dense fall of ashes. Every Roman villa had a solarium or sun porch.

Galen and Celsus recommended the sun bath, as did Avicenna in the tenth century.

Arthritis was treated with sun baths by Bonnet in the middle of the last century. Half a century later, Bernhard and Rollier began the systematic use of the sun bath and about the same time, sun treatment was instituted at Berck-Plage, on the Piccardy coast of France.

We owe our knowledge of the physics of light to the studies by Isaac Newton of the spectrum.

Finsen began the use of light in the treatment of lupus in the last decade of the nineteenth century.

The sun bath was first systematically employed in this country under medical supervision at the Battle Creek Sanitarium, in the year 1876.

The penetrating power of the luminous heat rays was accidentally discovered by the author in 1891, and immediate practical use was made of this fact in the application to therapeutics of the light from incandescent and arc lamps. Cabinets and other appliances constructed for the therapeutic use of light were shown at the Quadri-Centennial Exposition held in Chicago in 1893.

The year following the writer read a paper on the electric light bath before the American Electro-Therapeutic Association, and three years later, contributed by request (1897), a paper entitled, "The Use of Heat by a New Method" for *"Fortschritte der Hydrotherapie Festschrift zum Vierzigjährigen Doctorjubiläum des Prof. Dr. W. Winternitz,"* the first publication in German relating to the use of radiant heat.

The J. N. Adam Memorial Hospital at Perrysburg, New York, organized the first notable example of Rollier's sun and open air treatment of tuberculosis in this country.

Dr. E. Mayer and his colleagues of Saranac Lake have recently made important clinical studies of light therapy in cases of pulmonary tuberculosis and Dr. Mayer has written a compendious, almost encyclopedic, work on the light therapy of pulmonary tuberculosis.

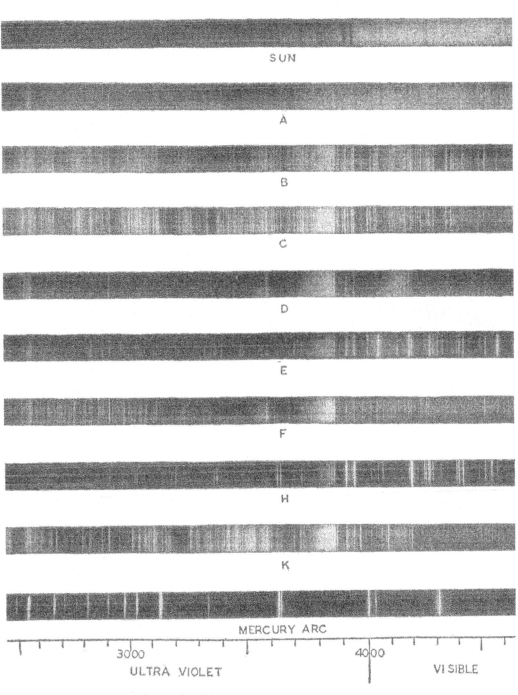

SUN

A

B

C

D

E

F

H

K

MERCURY ARC

30'00   40|00

ULTRA VIOLET   VISIBLE

SUN—Spectrogram of Bright Sunlight.

A—Spectrogram from Carbons Impregnated with Rare Earth Compounds. Powerful Erythema-Producing Rays. Resembles Sunlight.

B—Iron Carbons Similar to A but less intense.

C—Polymetallic Carbons. Wide Range of Ultra-Violet Rays.

D—Silicate Carbons. Rich in Red and Infra-Red Rays.

E—Strontium Carbons. Rich in Long Red, Highly Penetrating Rays.

F—Tungsten Carbons. Fairly Rich in Ultra-Violet Rays Though Less Intense than C Carbons.

H—Calcium Carbons. Yellow Light. Rich in Highly Penetrating Luminous and Infra-Red Rays.

K—Cobalt Carbons. Powerful Ultra-Violet Rays in the Near Ultra-Violet Region.

MERCURY ARC. Strong in Ultra-Violet Region. Weak in Penetrating Rays.

*These spectograms were obtained by the use of carbons made by the National Therapeutic Carbon Co.

SPECTROGRAMS

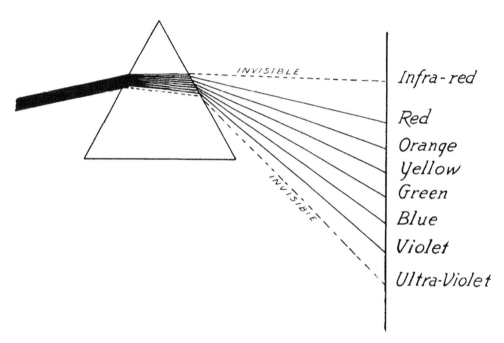

DISPERSION OF LIGHT RAYS BY A PRISM

The Physics of Light

Modern physicists regard light as a form of electro-magnetic energy which travels in straight lines or rays. Radiant energy manifests itself in a variety of forms of which light is only one, others being known as the X-ray, gamma rays, heat rays, wireless, etc., all being of the same intrinsic nature.

All the radiant forces travel through space at the same rate, a little more than 186,000 miles per second. They progress by a wave motion, the length of wave and the rate of wave movement differing with each of the various forms of radiant energy, although the rate of progression is the same for all.

Different Kinds of Light—The Spectrum

When white light is passed through a glass prism, it is decomposed. The several different kinds of rays of which it consists are separated by being refracted; that is, made to travel in diverging directions so that each of the different sorts of light rays may be separately studied. The broad band of colors into which the ray of white light is thus spread out is known as the *spectrum*. The central portion of the spectrum is brilliantly colored; this is known as the *visible spectrum*. It displays seven clearly defined colors which blend into many intermediate tints and hues, as displayed in the rainbow. The differences in color are due to difference in the frequency of vibration, as shown in the following table:

The Visible Spectrum

	Wave-length	Frequency (per second)
Red	6500 A.U.	462,000,000,000,000
Orange	6000 "	500,000,000,000,000
Yellow	5510 "	517,000,000,000,000
Green	5200 "	577,000,000,000,000
Blue	4750 "	638,000,000,000,000
Indigo	4400 "	680,000,000,000,000
Violet	4100 "	732,000,000,000,000

It is an interesting fact that the waves which produce the shortest visible violet light have a frequency rate about double that of red light. Thus, the visible spectrum comprises approximately one octave. As there are musical sounds so low on the one hand and so high pitched on the other as to be outside the range of the human ear though perhaps audible to other animals, so also with light rays; and we have an *invisible spectrum* on each side of the visible spectrum. The part beyond the red end of the visible spectrum is called the *infra-red,* discovered by Herschel (1800), who noted that mercury rose in a thermometer placed in this region where no rays were visible. Beyond the violet is the invisible *ultra-violet* spectrum discovered by Ritter and Wollaston (1803). These observers found that certain chemical effects such as the blackening of solutions of silver chloride, were produced in this region. The infra-red region extends for more than nine octaves below the red.

The longest infra-red rays are within four octaves of the Hertzian region, which includes the so-called wireless or radio waves. Thus gamma rays, X-rays, ultra-violet radiation, visible light, infra-red radiation, Hertzian or radio rays and even the long waves from commercial alternating currents are all included in the great gamut of electro-magnetic radiations. They are all essentially of the same nature. They all travel with the same velocity but differ in their frequency of vibration and wave length and differ to an extraordinary degree in their physical properties and in their effects upon the human body and hence in their therapeutic properties and uses.

There are several means by which these various rays may be separated. For example, a spherical flask filled with a solution of iodin in disulphid of carbon, filters out both the luminous and the chemical rays while transmitting the heat rays. Such a flask, the contents of which appear to the eye to be absolutely opaque, may be used as a burning glass, and a bit of cotton set on fire by focusing upon it the invisible heat rays. A solution of alum permits luminous rays to pass through it, but absorbs heat rays.

It is only necessary to filter the light through red or yellow glass to eliminate the ultra-violet rays. The photographer utilizes this fact in the construction of his dark room. Ordinary window glass excludes the greater portion of the chemical rays. Pure quartz glass transmits a large percentage of the ultra-violet rays. Several new kinds of glass have recently been perfected which transmit more or less completely the ultra-violet rays.

The accompanying spectrograms show clearly the relative value of some of these new glasses among which may be especially mentioned vita glass, corex and helioglass. Coblenz has shown that some of these new glasses deteriorate rapidly.

The Gamut of Radiant Energy

	Angström Units*
Cosmic rays (Millikan rays)	0 0004
Gamma rays, short	.07 to 1.3
X-rays	0.10 to 200.00
Ultra-violet, extreme	200 to 2,000
Ultra-violet, middle	2,000 to 3,000
Ultra-violet, near	3,000 to 3,900
Visible rays, shortest	3,900
Visible rays, longest	8,100
Infra-red, inner, penetrating	8,100 to 10,000
Infra-red, outer, non-penetrating	200,000
Infra-red, longest	3,000,000
Hertzian, shortest	20,000,000
Hertzian, wireless	4,000,000 to 200,000,000—13 miles
Commercial alternating current	50,000,000,000 or 3,000 miles

Regional Classification of Radiant Energy

The whole gamut of light rays from the longest infra-red which have been spectroscopically studied, to the shortest gamma rays consists of more than 20 octaves of which visible light constitutes but 1 octave, with 9 octaves below in the infra-red and 16 octaves in the ultra-violet and short wave region.

---

*An Angström unit is 1/10,000,000 of a milligram or 1/250,000,000 of an inch.

Light from Different Sources Compared

The light of the electric arc is very similar to that of the sun. An ordinary arc-lamp presents a light-radiating surface of about one-tenth of an inch square. The temperature of the arc is so extremely high that the energy thrown off is practically the same as that emitted by an equal area of the outer surface of the sun.

Excepting sunlight and the magnesium light, no light is so effective chemically as the white flame carbon arc. The light of a powerful arc lamp is as potent as sunlight in its action on photographic plates.

According to the photometric investigations of Vogel, sunlight is eight to fourteen times more powerful than diffused daylight with a clear sky. The electric arc light, 1,000 candle power, at a distance of one and a half meters (five feet), is four times as powerful as diffused daylight in November with a clear sky.

Vogel found that a Shuckert reflector with 60-ampere current was sufficient to make a black photographic reproduction in fifteen seconds, while daylight in November, using the same materials, required three minutes, or twelve times as long. Strebel confirms this finding.

The chemical effect of the arc light is greatly heightened by the use of suitable reflectors, giving considerably more powerful effects than with lenses, and without the danger of producing burn blisters.

Light from an incandescent lamp contains a very small proportion of ultra-violet rays: first, because of the comparatively low temperature at which the light is produced; second, because the incandescent filament is enclosed within a globe of ordinary glass, which does not transmit the shorter ultra-violet rays.

The great difference in the properties of the incandescent lamp and the arc lamp was well shown in an address by Sir James Dewar on the subject of "Flame," delivered before the Royal Institution of London. By careful analysis of the rays obtained from different incandescent sources, the distinguished physicist demonstrated that of the total rays emitted by a candle

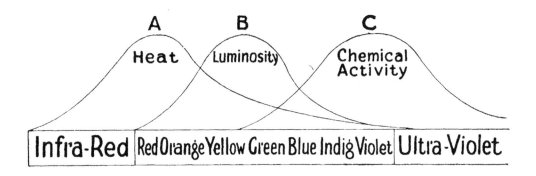

GROUPING OF LIGHT RAYS ACCORDING TO THEIR THERAPEUTIC
ACTIVITY

DIAGRAMS SHOWING RANGE AND PENETRATING POWER OF THE SEVERAL
CLASSES OF RAYS

flame, 98% are thermic and 2% luminous. The filament of an incandescent lamp throws off rays of which 1% to 3% only are luminous, 97% to 99% being thermic or heat rays. The arc lamp, on the other hand, gives only 80% of heat rays.

Infra-red rays are given off from all heated objects. The heat radiated from a steam pipe or other non-luminous sources has little or practically no penetrating power. A temperature close to incandescence is necessary for the emission of penetrating infra-red rays.

Sunlight

The light energy received from the sun reaches us in a modified condition, a considerable proportion of the shorter waves being filtered out by the atmosphere. As it reaches us, the sun's rays have the following composition:

Temperature (absolute)	Per cent Radiation
Infra-red rays	80 per cent
Luminous rays	19 per cent
Ultra-violet rays	1 per cent

Sunlight is much less rich in ultra-violet rays than is light from some other sources, especially heated metals. The deep study of the sun's rays which has been made by physicists within the last few years, has thrown a great flood of light upon this subject which is of precious value to clinicians. A very important practical fact is the great variability of the intensity of the sunlight and especially of the ultra-violet rays, an element of highest interest from a therapeutic standpoint.

Color Scale of Temperature

Color	Temperature (Degrees Fahr.)
Incipient red heat	932-1022
Dark red heat	1202-1382
Bright red heat	1562-1742
Yellowish red heat	1922-2102
Incipient white heat	2282-2462
White heat	2642-2822

Luminous and Non-Luminous Heat Rays

All the visible rays of the spectrum, red, orange, yellow, green, blue, indigo, and violet, are thermic and actinic as well as luminous. Luminosity centers in the yellow, heat in the red, running over into the inner infra-red, and the actinic in the violet, extending into the ultra-violet, as shown in the accompanying illustration after Burk and Sonne. In general, luminous heat rays are more penetrating than the non-luminous. Sunlight contains a much larger proportion of these highly penetrating heat rays than does the arc light (sun $33\frac{1}{3}$ per cent luminous rays, arc light 15 to 20 per cent). The incandescent light gives only 3 to 5 per cent luminous rays.

Factors Which Influence the Intensity of Sunlight

The height of the sun affects the intensity of the rays.

At 10° the earth receives 20 per cent
At 30° the earth receives 56 per cent
At 50° the earth receives 69 per cent
At 90° the earth receives 75 per cent

In Madrid, Spain, there are nearly 3,000 hours of sunshine in a year. In Scotland, hardly 200. At the summit of Ben Nevis, the highest mountain in Great Britain, 726 hours.

Ultra-Violet Light

The difference between the longest and the shortest ultra-violet rays is much greater than that between the violet and red rays of the visible spectrum. The shorter ultra-violet rays in some respects resemble the X-rays.

These invisible ultra-violet rays are highly refrangible and hence are widely dispersed. Their refrangibility is so great that, according to Wood, there is in full sunlight no shade for ultra-violet light.

The ultra-violet rays possess very active chemical properties. They readily produce, without heat, chemical changes which when caused by heat require a temperature of more than 1,000° F. When allowed to fall upon metals, ultra-violet rays produce effects similar to those produced by the powerful rays of radium, causing the atoms to throw off negative electrons. It has been suggested that this is the explanation of the remarkable effect of ultra-violet light upon animal life, particularly its remarkable effect in causing the assimilation of calcium and other mineral substances.

Highly heated bodies always emit ultra-violet rays along with other light and heat rays. The higher the temperature the shorter are the waves emitted and hence the greater the proportion of ultra-violet rays. The maximum of intensity of ultra-violet light is found at the wave length of 2,940 A (Saidman), the production of which requires a temperature of more than 12,000° Fahrenheit.

The amount of ultra-violet radiation is influenced by the nature of the heated body as well as by the temperature. The most intense ultra-violet rays are produced by the heating of metals, most of which give rise to a great number of rays. Because of the large number of rays none have the highest degree of intensity, the energy being divided up among the different rays. There are, however, a few metals which produce only a small number of rays, which are in consequence of much greater intensity.

This fact is of great practical importance in the selection of electrodes. For example, tungsten and iron produce a light rich in ultra-violet radiation, but electrodes containing magnesium, cadmium or aluminum are preferable because the ultra-violet radiation produced is concentrated in the region 2800A to 3100A, which is most active therapeutically.

Natural Sources of Ultra-Violet Light

The amount of ultra-violet light found in the sunlight varies greatly with the season and the time of day. The variation due to changes in the season is from 1 to 10. The lowest intensity is in January.

The following table gives the comparative intensity of the ultra-violet element of the sunlight in different months of the year:

January	0.1	July	1.0
March	0.3	August	0.9
April	0.5	September	0.8
May	0.8	October	0.6
June	0.9	December	0.2

Daily Variation of Ultra-Violet Rays

The variation of the intensity of the ultra-violet rays of the sunlight at different hours of the day may be 40 to 1. The larger part of the ultra-violet rays of the sunlight, including all the shorter rays, is absorbed by the ozone and other elements of the atmosphere. According to Duclaux, the shorter rays are absorbed by ammonia. If it were not for the protection thus afforded by the earth's atmosphere, human life on this planet would doubtless be impossible. In high mountain regions the intensity of the ultra-violet rays is greater because the atmosphere is clearer and its density less. There is also in these elevated regions less variation between summer and winter in the intensity of the sunlight. The ultra-violet rays of Alpine regions are as intense in winter as in inland regions at sea level in July.

Variation of the Intensity of Sunlight, Midday Being Taken as Unity

Time	Total Light Intensity
8:00 A. M.	0.4
10:00 A. M.	0.7
Midday	1.0
2:00 P. M.	0.9
4:00 P. M.	0.6
6:00 P. M.	0.4

The direct rays from the sun are often less intense than the diffused light reflected from the sky. This is especially important at the seashore, where the reflection of light from the sky may be four times as great as at an altitude of 5,000 feet. While direct light from the sun increases with altitude, the reflected light decreases.

The diffusion of the ultra-violet rays is very much greater than that of other light rays. The amount of red rays received from the sun and that received from the sky are equal, while in the case of violet rays (.4220 A), seven times as much is received from the sky as from the sun direct.

The amount of ultra-violet light is also influenced by reflection from white clouds, snow, sand and the surface of the water. The sea and snow reflect the most, sand the least.

In making studies of the intensity of the ultra-violet rays of the sunlight at Biskra, an oasis in the Sahara Desert, in the months of January and February, 1926, the writer was surprised to find the intensity of the ultra-violet rays much less than he expected. Several hours' exposure to the sun was necessary to produce even slight erythema. Measurements of the intensity of the light made by means of Bordier's test paper, showed a degree of intensity at midday comparable with that of Michigan in early fall.

Making Ultra-Violet Rays Visible

The short waves of ultra-violet light may become luminous by contact with certain substances by which the short, invisible waves are converted into the longer, luminous waves. Thus, ultra-violet light becomes luminous in the iridescence of kerosene oil, solutions of quinine and many other substances which absorb and retain ultra-violet rays from the sun or other sources. This explains the interesting experiment in which invisible writing made with a solution of quinin may be photographed as successfully as if it were made with visible ink. These invisible chemical rays are thus able to render visible many things which would otherwise remain undiscoverable. The curious fact has been pointed out that the eruption of smallpox may through these rays be made visible in a photograph before it can be discovered by the naked eye.

The art of photography is based upon the influence of the chemical rays upon various chemical compounds. The photographer's films are extremely sensitive to the action of these rays, and hence must be carefully shielded from their influence.

Luminescence—Fluorescence—Phosphorescence

While intense heat is the usual source of light, there are numerous other sources of light rays, such as luminous fishes, fireflies, certain micro-organisms, friction, chemical action, such as the oxidation of phosphorus, and certain electrical phenomena. Light of this sort is not accompanied by an appreciable degree of heat, and is known as *luminescence*.

Certain insects which lack the color sense or are color-blind, are able to see by means of the ultra-violet radiation, which causes *fluorescence* in the crystal ball of the insect's eye.

When solids are heated, light begins to appear as a dull, red color only when the temperature 932° F. has been reached; but certain bodies give off light at a temperature of 400° or 500°. This phenomenon is known as *thermo-luminescence*.

Certain substances possess the curious property of being able to transform short, non-visible rays into longer, visible rays. When the light is thrown off as rapidly as it is received, it is known as *fluorescence*. Screens made of substances which possess this property render very great service in X-ray examinations by making visible the action of the heart, diaphragm, stomach and other internal organs.

Among well-known fluorescent substances are eosin, fluorescein, fluorin.

A few substances, zinc, cadmium and the sulphides of the alkaline earths, store up short-length, invisible light rays and later give off the longer rays of visible light. This is known as *phosphorescence*.

Artificial Sources of Ultra-Violet Light

Ordinary lamps and candles do not emit any considerable amount of ultra-violet radiation. Disrupted spark discharges produced between electrodes by a high tension current arc very rich in ultra-violet rays. The luminous discharges in vacuum tubes are a feeble source of ultra-violet light. Burning magnesium produces ultra-violet rays having a length of 2,800 A. The most intense rays of the oxyhydrogen light have a wave length of 3,300 A. A tungsten filament lamp produces rays having waves

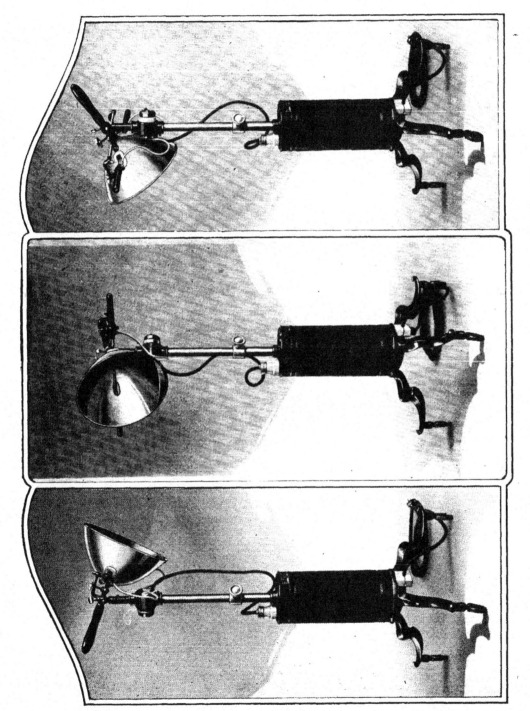

THE ORIGINAL CARBON-ARC THERAPEUTIC LAMP (KELLOGG)

not shorter than 3,700 A. and hence are not efficient sources of ultra-violet light even when a quartz globe is employed.

For practical purposes the carbon arc light is the most efficient source of ultra-violet as well as luminous and infra-red rays. The efficiency of the arc light is due to the high temperature attained by the tip of the negative electrode and the crater in the positive electrode.

The efficiency of the arc light increases with increase of the distance between the tips of the electrodes; that is, the greater the length of the arc the greater the amount of radiation emitted.

The volume and intensity of the arc are increased by the presence of metals in the electrodes which create the so-called *flaming arc*. When metallic electrodes are employed with a direct current, the positive electrode should be placed beneath the negative. With pure carbon electrodes, the positive is placed above the negative. This arrangement produces the greatest efficiency.

The color of the arc depends upon the metal employed. Iron produces a blue-violet flame, copper blue, aluminum and manganese, greenish.

The amount of light produced will depend upon the size of the electrode and the quantity and voltage of the current. An arc light with polymetallic electrodes produces intense ultra-violet rays of wave length 2,568 A. to 2,852 A. The Finsen arc gives ultra-violet rays ranging from 2,500 A. to 2,900 A.

The quartz, or mercury-vapor lamp, is an efficient source of ultra-violet light. The air-cooled lamp produces ultra-violet rays of the longer wave length and is best suited for general applications. The water-cooled, or Kromayer lamp, produces the shorter ultra-violet rays, the so-called far ultra-violet, and is better adapted for intensive local applications. In general the arc light is to be preferred for the reason that it produces an ample amount of ultra-violet light while at the same time producing a flood of the more highly penetrating luminous rays and short infra-red rays.

The arc between metal electrodes, the flaming arc and the mercury arc, are the most powerful sources of ultra-violet rays. Finsen found the iron electrode arc to be 50 times as powerful as the carbon-arc. The flaming arc is a highly active source of the ultra-violet rays because of the radiation from vaporized metals as well as from the electrodes.

The Reflection of Ultra-Violet Radiation

The best reflector for ultra-violet rays is silicon (75%). Aluminum and magnalium are next in order. Nickel and platinum reflect less than half the ultra-violet radiation received, while silver reflects only 4% of the most useful ultra-violet rays. Snow and water are good reflectors of ultra-violet rays.

Infra-Red Rays

All heated bodies give rise to infra-red rays. This is true of both luminous and non-luminous heated bodies. Both sunlight and the arc light are highly efficient sources of infra-red rays. The idea that the rays from non-luminous heated bodies have a greater penetrating power than those from luminous heated bodies is wholly without foundation and is based upon gross ignorance of the physics of light. Both the profession and the public have been shamefully imposed upon by manufacturers who have exploited the infra-red idea in the sale of appliances possessing less therapeutic efficiency than an ordinary hot sand bag or a hot water bottle. The very best possible source for infra-red rays is the sun or an efficient arc lamp.

The great French physicist Fourtier, and afterward Professor Tyndall, showed that the dark heat rays have not the penetrating power of the rays of shorter wave length which are found in the visible spectrum. Dark heat rays, that is, the rays given off by ordinary non-luminous heated bodies such as heat from a stove or a steam coil, are not even capable of passing through ordinary glass. This is the explanation of hot-bed heat. The short-wave heat rays of the sunlight penetrate the glass roof of the hot-bed and are absorbed by the earth. The dark heat rays which are radiated back from the earth cannot penetrate the glass and so the heat accumulates in the enclosed space. Langley saw the heat in such a space exposed to the sun's rays rise to 235° F. when the outside temperature was 59° F. The atmosphere acts in the same way in relation to the earth as glass to a hot-bed because of the carbonic acid gas, ozone, ammonia, and water vapor which it contains.

The Physiologic Effects of Light

Although the influence of light upon animal and vegetable life has long been known in a general way, it is only within a comparatively short time that the subject has been studied with sufficient care to place the therapeutic utilization of light upon a sound and rational basis. The experiments of Arloing, d'Arsonval, Geisler, Paul Bert, DuBois, Graber, and especially Finsen, Reyn and Rollier, Gauvain and Leonard Hill have contributed most important facts toward the solution of the many interesting questions connected with this subject.

When closely analyzed, these effects may be shown to belong to two classes: first, those which are due to the action of the ultra-violet rays; and second, those which are due to the heat radiations. Practically, these effects are always more or less combined, but for clearness it is well to consider separately the two classes of effects.

Light a Vital Stimulant

The classic experiments of Finsen, some of which the writer had the opportunity to witness, having several times visited the Light Institute at Copenhagen (1899, 1902 and 1926), clearly demonstrated that the actinic rays are a powerful excitant of vital activity, and hence promote to the highest degree all the processes of animal life and energy. This was a discovery of the highest importance—one which explains many facts of common observation which had before been inexplicable.

The chemical ray is the source of the energy which enables the plant to elaborate in its leaves, under the influence of the sunlight, the various products necessary for its development. Vegetable structures consist, in fact, of simple elements held together in complex molecules by the energy derived from the sunlight. Under the magic influence of these miracle-working rays, the elements found in earth, air and water are organized into

23

molecular groups, some comprising thousands of atoms, the breaking up of which, as the result of vital activity, liberates the light energy employed in holding together these organic unities, permitting the energy thus set free to manifest itself in muscular and mental effort, and various other forms of vital work.

To be able to harness this force, to control it, and to focus it upon any desired organ or function of the body, is one of the newest and greatest triumphs of modern therapeutics.

The Effects of Light Upon Plant Life

Siemens in 1880 published a detailed account of experiments for the purpose of determining the influence of light upon vegetation. The following may be deduced from his results:

1. The electric light is efficacious in producing chlorophyl in the leaves of plants, and in promoting growth.

2. An electric center of light, equal to 1,400 candles, placed at a distance of two meters from growing plants, appeared to be equal in effect to average daylight at this season of the year (March); but more economical effects can be attained by more powerful light centers.

3. Carbonic acid and nitrogenous compounds generated in diminutive quantities in the electric arc produce no sensible deleterious effects upon plants enclosed in the same space.

4. Some plants appear not to require a period of rest during any part of the twenty-four hours of the day, but make increased and vigorous progress if subjected during the daytime to sunlight and during the night to the arc light, showing that it is a substitute for sunlight, or identical with it.

Experiments made at the Boyce-Thompson laboratory at Yonkers, N. Y., have shown that under the influence of continuous light, sunlight during the day time and electric light at night, plants may be made to grow and mature at more than double the usual rate.

Recent observations respecting the influence of light on the movements of plants show that in some instances the ultra-violet rays are most active, in others the infra-red.

The Effects of Colored Light on Plants

Some years ago the writer conducted a series of experiments in the growing of plants, with some striking results. Seeds of various sorts were planted in boxes covered with cloths of uniform fabric but of different colors—white, red, green, blue, and black. The effects of color, as shown in the growth and appearance of the plants, were very marked.

In one experiment, one box was left uncovered. The seeds in a box covered with black cloth, germinated more quickly than the seeds in the other boxes, and these plants appeared above the earth sooner than the others. This was attributed to the fact that black absorbs all the rays of light and heat; the air and soil in this box were warmer than in the other boxes.

As the plants developed, a marked difference in the color of the leaves was very quickly recognizable. The leaves growing under the white cloth were almost as green as those of plants growing without any covering. The same was true of those beneath the yellow cloth. The plants growing under the red cloth showed slight traces of green color, but those under the black, dark blue and dark green, showed no trace of green. In the plants grown under black, the chlorophyl was evidently wholly lacking. The experiment was repeated indoors, with results identical with those obtained outdoors in the open sunshine.

Since these experiments were made, we have learned of observations by Bowles, Bonbuoff and Paul Schmidt, which show that ordinary cloth is more or less pervious to ultra-violet rays. This fact explains the presence of freckles on covered parts (Bernhard). The writer's experiments demonstrated, however, that the amount of light which reaches the skin through the ordinary clothing, is quite inadequate. Our experiments show clearly that the color of clothing is a matter of importance, and that the amount of light which comes in contact with the skin may be modified by the color of the fabrics worn as well as by their texture. When white clothing is worn in the sunlight, the body is bathed in light, notwithstanding the fact that it is covered. When dark clothing is worn, all light is excluded from all portions of the skin. In other words, when we wear dark clothing, we live in the dark both day and night; whereas, when white is worn during the hours of daylight, we "walk in the light."

The influence of color on the absorption of light through the clothing, as demonstrated by our experiment, is, we believe, a new observation and one the importance of which is such as to justify serious consideration.

Invalids and Children Should Wear White Clothes

In sanitariums and hospitals, particularly in sanitoria for tuberculosis, the wearing of white clothing should be made a regulation practice.

The value of sunlight in the treatment of disease is now so well established, every pains should be taken to secure to every sick person the full benefits of the sun's rays. Thin, white clothing permits the transmission of a sufficient amount of light to influence nutrition to a marked degree. Invalids should never be kept in dark rooms nor allowed to remain constantly in the shade or behind ordinary glass windows. It is not to be forgotten that living in a room lighted by ordinary glass is equivalent to living in a dungeon so far as the ultra-violet rays are concerned, for window glass almost completely excludes this precious source of life and energy.

Besides wearing white clothing, invalids should spend several hours a day in the open air exposed to the open sky. The direct rays of the sun are of the highest value, but the light reflected from the sky and from clouds is also beneficial. Even under the shade of a tree or other shelter, if some portion of the sky is visible, really beneficial effects may be received.

Growing children, especially, should be clothed in white or light colored garments. Children need light to enable them to grow and to form healthy tissues as much as do plants. Plants grown in the dark are frail and slender. Their tissues are tender and lack toughness of fiber. This is why we like our celery blanched. Children raised in the shade are rickety, puny and an easy prey to germs, especially the germs of tuberculosis, and they are likely to die early. Two-thirds of the population of the United States live in cities and nearly all are suffering from lack of contact of the sun with the skin. Simply exposing the skin of the face and hands to the sun is not sufficient. The skin area varies, of course, with the size of the body, but totals for the average adult fifteen to twenty square feet. The skin area of the face and hands is less than one-tenth of the total.

It is evident, then, that those who wear heavy or dark colored clothing get little actual contact with the sun's rays, even though they may spend most of their time in the open air. Small children ought to wear as little clothing as possible in the summer season so as to allow their bodies to become well browned in contact with the sun and air.

It is the conviction of the writer that the general adoption of white clothing, both summer and winter, would favorably influence, to a marked degree, the health of the nation. Growing children, invalids, and persons compelled to live indoors, would be especially benefited by the wearing of white clothing. The famous Grecian philosopher Pythagoras, dressed in white clothing, as did his pupils and followers. The famous Count Rumford wore white clothing for the very reason given above. The natives of all hot countries wear white clothing, as do the polar bear and the fox of the Arctic regions.

The Arc Light Acts Like Sunlight

In plants, chlorophyl pigment can only be formed in the light. Plants and plant parts grown in the dark have no chlorophyl, but are pale yellow in color. The yellow rays are needed for chlorophyl (Freund). The quantity of light need not be large. A light barely strong enough for the reading of large print enables sprouting plants to grow dark green (Wiesner). Plants grown in the dark have abnormally long internodes and leaf stems.

Experiments by Hervé-Mangon demonstrated that the arc light is capable of causing a development of chlorophyl and of inducing heliotropism (bending toward the source of light). Prillieux showed that the arc light is capable of promoting assimilation in plants.

Chemical and Protective Effect of Ultra-Violet Light

The powerful effects of ultra-violet rays are shown in the chemical changes produced in various substances. For example, when milk is exposed to ultra-violet rays for a few minutes it acquires an unpleasant flavor. Cane sugar exposed to the rays becomes yellow. Hydrochloric acid, which requires a very high degree of heat to decompose it, breaks down under the influence of ultra-violet rays.

The ultra-violet rays may possibly exert a protective influence over our planet. Saidman recalls the fact that when there was a widespread fear of danger to be incurred by the passage of the earth through the tail of Halley's comet, the chemist Bertholet quieted the public apprehension by assurance that the poisonous cyanogen with which the comet's tail was charged would be destroyed by the ultra-violet rays of the sun, so that no harm would result, which proved to be the case.

Effects of the Ultra-Violet or Chemical Rays on Plants

The experiments made by Finsen and others show that chemical and thermic rays exert a decidedly different influence upon plant growth. The ultra-violet rays increase flowering, while the heat rays enhance the aroma. The action of the sunflower and other heliotropic plants in bending toward the sun, shows the powerful influence of light upon life processes as manifested in plants. Plants, however, appear to be subject to damage from excess of the ultra-violet rays just as animals suffer sunstroke from excessive exposure to the sun.

Light Destroys Bacteria

While light in general is favorable to the growth of plant life, the opposite is true as regards bacteria. All known pathogenic bacteria are killed by light, and the same is true of pathogenic protozoa. In general, the vegetative forms are most sensitive to light and are the most easily killed; but in some species, the spores are more susceptible to the destructive influence of light rays.

Finsen found that bright sunlight killed plate cultures of *bacillus prodigiosus* after an hour-and-a-half exposure. It required eight to nine hours' exposure and an electric arc lamp of 25 amperes to kill a plate culture of this same bacillus at a distance of 75 c. m. from the carbon arc. Finsen then tried the effect of concentrated light upon the *bacillus prodigiosus* and the typhoid bacillus. IIe found that concentrated sunlight killed the organisms fifteen times more quickly than ordinary sunlight, and that the influence of concentrated arc light was still more powerful.

Procaccini exposed to sunlight sewer water containing 300,-000 to 420,000 bacteria per cubic centimeter. After a day's exposure the water was sterile.

Bacteria are readily killed by light at the surface of the soil, although twenty inches below the surface they may resist destruction for four or five months.

Dieudonné's observations showed that bacteria were killed in half an hour by direct sunlight, in six hours by diffused daylight, and in eight hours by an electric arc light (900 candle-power). Bang showed that the unconcentrated light from a thirty-ampere arc lamp will kill a surface layer of tubercle bacilli at a distance of thirty centimeters (twelve inches) in six minutes. The strongest bactericidal sun's rays are absorbed in the air; thus an arc lamp is found to be a valuable, practical source of bactericidal rays.

Von Jansen inserted between the light rays and the bacteria a piece of skin 1.2 millimeters thick, and found that destruction of bacteria occurred in one and one-fourth hours. With skin 1.5 millimeters thick the bacteria were no longer destroyed.

There is a difference of opinion as to how the bacteria are killed. Some authorities claim that it is the direct influence of the ultra-violet rays; others hold that the destruction of bacteria is due to the changes induced in the tissues by the light.

The incandescent light has very slight effect in direct bactericidal action. Any favorable influence of incandescent light treatment on bacterial diseases must be explained by the indirect action of light rays in stimulating metabolism and in increasing leucocytosis and phagocytosis. Incandescent lamps give out very few chemically active rays.

Ultra-Violet Light Especially Destructive to Bacteria

That ultra-violet light will destroy bacteria has long been known and has been made of practical service as a means of purification of water. The rays most active are those which have a wave length of less than 3,000 A. The shorter waves have the greater efficiency.

The length of time required for the destruction of various organisms differs greatly. Most pathogenic organisms are killed in ten to twenty seconds, while yeasts and molds and the tetanus bacillus require a full minute. The typhoid bacillus and the organisms which give rise to dysentery and cholera, as well as the colon bacillus, are quickly destroyed by the ultra-violet light. Some bacteria which resist strong solutions of germicides, and even a prolonged boiling temperature, are quickly killed by exposure to light.

Experiments made with tetanus germs showed that they were more readily killed by direct sunlight than by a one to one-thousand solution of bichloride of mercury. The virulence of many pathogenic germs is attenuated if they are kept in the light. Diffused light acting during a long period is destructive to germs, but nearly all bacteria perish quickly when exposed to the direct influence of the sun's rays. The germicidal property of the chemical ray makes it without doubt the most powerful of nature's disinfecting agencies. If it were not for this agency, the earth would quickly become uninhabitable through the rapid development of death-dealing organisms.

Koch observed that ultra-violet rays destroy not only bacteria but bacterial toxins, and the venoms of serpents.

Infra-Red Rays Destroy Bacteria

Weisnner has demonstrated that infra-red rays as well as the ultra-violet, possess powerful germicidal properties. He regarded the infra-red rays as fully equal, if not superior, to the ultra-violet rays in their bactericidal properties.

The Effects of Light Upon Animal Life

The development of many animals is dependent upon light. Frog spawn die in an opaque flask, while in a transparent glass vessel they develop normally. Tadpoles develop more slowly in the dark than in the light (Edwards).

Finsen observed that the red corpuscles in tadpoles were contracted and became rounder under the influence of light.

Finsen also noted that the growth of the nails, hair and other epidermal tissues is encouraged by light and hindered by darkness. In his clinic he had noted that patients and nurses who work for a long time with powerful arc lights grow more hair on the arms, which are much exposed to the action of light.

According to Harrington and Leaming, red light (short-length heat waves) is most favorable to the movements of the amœba, both the violet and the yellow rays impeding its movements. Englemann observed contraction of the amœba on sudden exposure to light, and rapid relaxation of the amœba when suddenly exposed to darkness.

Loeb found that the more refrangible rays encourage the growth of polyps. The red rays have the same effect as total darkness.

Flies' eggs develop more rapidly under glass admitting only the chemical rays than under glass admitting luminous or heat rays (Beclard). Maggots develop more quickly in pieces of meat exposed to the light than in meat kept in the dark (Gadneff).

The activity of the silkworm is encouraged by violet light (Guarinoni).

Light without heat causes the iris to contract in the eye of amphibia and fishes. This happens in any case, even when the retina has been removed and when the eye has been extracted some time before (Brown-Sequard). This phenomenon is probably due to direct irritation of the muscle by light. Harless, in studying human corpses thirty hours after death, observed distinct contraction of the pupil of the eye when exposed to light. Englemann also showed that light causes the rods and cones of the retina to shorten, while darkness lengthens them.

It is a matter of common knowledge among farmers that domestic animals develop better in well-lighted sheds than in dark ones. The same principle is recognized with reference to the development of young children.

Parasitic organisms do not thrive in the sunlight. Not only pathogenic protozoa but fleas are killed by the sunlight. In hot countries, the clothing is cleared of fleas by exposure to the sun.

Influence of Colored Light on Human Beings

It has long been known that the color of living rooms and the rooms occupied by patients in hospitals has a decided influence upon mental states and sense of well-being. This fact has generally been attributed to the psychologic influence of colors because of their associations, black and somber colors suggesting funerals and so having a depressing effect, while bright colors have a cheering influence because of their association with festivity and gaiety.

Recent observations, however, suggest very definitely that the effects recognized may be physical rather than mental and that they may be explained on purely physical grounds. It is known that light rays are totally reflected by white and totally absorbed by black. Red, blue, green and other colors, absorb all rays except those of their own color.

It is evident, then, that when light enters a room the walls of which are dark in color, a considerable part of the incoming light is absorbed by the walls, and a person occupying such a room will not only be living under a shadow, but under a very dark shadow, and will be almost wholly deprived of the influence of light.

On the other hand, a person occupying a room the walls of which are white, or nearly white, and hence which reflect instead of absorbing a large part of the luminous rays, while he also will be living in the shadow, will nevertheless be surrounded by such a volume of reflected or diffused light that the absence of direct sunlight will be in a large degree compensated for.

Experiments made by the writer have clearly demonstrated that the varying effects of light are the result of very tangible differences in the action of different colors in relation to the rays of light.

One experiment consisted in growing plants in chambers the walls of which were painted different colors: white, black, yellow, red, green and blue. Light was admitted into the chambers in such a way that it could reach the growing plants only after having been reflected from the chamber walls. The arrangement employed can easily be understood from the accompanying cut.

Plants grown in the black chamber showed no chlorophyl in their leaves. The plants grown in the blue chamber showed a slight trace of green. Those in the green chamber showed a trifle more color than the blue, but only a very faint, greenish tint. In the red box, the plants were green, but very pale. In the yellow and white boxes, the plants had the natural green color of oats grown in the open.

This experiment shows clearly that dark walls absorb from the light rays something which is essential to the life processes of plants, and since it is known that cell life—protoplasm, whether animal or vegetable—is essentially alike in its fundamental requirements, it is a reasonable conclusion that human life, as well as plant life, must be definitely and materially influenced by the color of the light-reflecting surfaces with which they are surrounded. It may be true especially of human beings who spend their lives indoors, such as teachers, students, professional men and persons engaged in business or scientific pursuits which keep them within walls.

Thousands of people, especially those of the well-to-do classes, are shut up for months, and even years, in dark-walled chambers into which the direct rays of the sun never penetrate. Such places are dangerous habitats.

Sun-illumined air is different from air which has not had the magneto-electric touch of the solar beams.

Graber observed that the earthworm, which habitually lives in the dark, when placed in a box half of which was covered with a red glass and the other half with a violet glass, at once placed itself under the protection of the red glass, toward which it behaved the same as toward total darkness. Although we are ordinarily unconscious of the fact, there is no doubt that our life processes are influenced—to a degree far greater than we are able to appreciate or comprehend—by these subtle emanations from the sun which are known as the chemical rays. We may, indeed, be influenced by still more subtle emanations from those far-away suns which we call the fixed stars; so there may have been something more than poetry in the question of the ancient sage, "Canst thou bind the sweet influences of the Pleiades?" The discovery of the "cosmic ray" by Milliken reveals ground for support of this conjecture.

Effects of the Ultra-Violet Rays on the Skin (Solar Erythema)

Nearly half a century ago Charcot suggested that sunburn, or solar erythema, might be due to the ultra-violet rays. Wilde observed that a so-called sunburn is not a burn at all, since it does not appear at once but comes some hours after exposure. Finsen furnished the scientific proof that a sunburn is simply an erythema resulting from an irritation set up by the ultra-violet rays. This phenomenon, which is quite too familiar to require description, affords most positive evidence of the potency of the chemical rays. Charcot, Widmark, Bowles and others have shown that the dermatitis produced by the electric arc light (light-burn) is also due to the action of the ultra-violet rays.

The ultra-violet rays which cause erythema and tanning are those of wave lengths 3200 to 2800 A. The shorter or far ultra-violet waves do not cause either erythema or pigmentation.

All persons are not equally sensitive to this influence of the chemical rays. Brunettes suffer less than do blondes. Negroes and other dark-skinned races are largely exempt from this unpleasant effect of the sun's rays. Lower animals as well as human beings are sensitive to the chemical rays, white cows being subject to sunburn the same as white-skinned men, while red and black cows are exempt.

Cows which are spotted red and white, or black and white, are subject to sunburn on the white spots and not on the dark spots. The curious fact has been observed that certain light-colored animals, especially cows or pigs, are more subject to sunburn after feeding on buckwheat. The reason for this has been supposed to be the development in the blood of some peculiar substance derived from the food or developed under the influence of light.

Pigmentation of the skin, or tanning, follows repeated or prolonged exposure to the influence of light, either with or without solar erythema. The cause of this darkening of the skin is the increase of pigment material through stimulation of the pigment cells of the skin. Bruecke and others have proved that the pigmentation of the skin is due to local action of the actinic rays on the skin, and not to the heat rays. In connection with solar erythema, there is doubtless also a disintegration of blood cells and the deposit of pigment from this source following sunburn. Sunburn usually occurs but once in persons who are taking a course of light applications, but to this rule there are occasional exceptions. The purpose of this increased pigment in the skin is protection. Even mulattoes have a much darker complexion when exposed to the sun in the summer time than in the winter season. In the South Sea Islands, when the natives are obliged to expose their naked bodies to the sun's rays for some time, they protect themselves from unpleasant effects by smearing their skins with black pigment.

The effects of ultra-violet rays upon the skin are much interfered with by even a very thin layer of fat. This is not true of mineral oils. For this reason the skin should be thoroughly cleansed before making a light application. A hot fomentation or friction of the skin just before a light application decidedly increases its effects. Equally good effects are produced by an application of the photophore or the infra-red light. If a short, cold application is made after heating the skin, the reaction produced creates a condition of the skin circulation which is the best possible preparation for a light application.

A Light Erythema is Not a Burn

It is to be clearly understood that a photo erythema is not a burn. A photo erythema differs from a burn in several particulars: First, the effects of a burn appear immediately, while the erythema resulting from an application of light makes its appearance some hours later. A second very essential difference is found in the fact that a photo erythema does not destroy the skin structures even when the reaction is very intense unless a highly intensive application has been made with the deliberate intention of producing destruction of tissue.

The erythema produced by a light application, even when very intense, should never be spoken of as a burn. This conveys a highly erroneous impression which gives rise to unnecessary apprehension of injury. The writer has never known of any permanent injury to be produced even by the most severe photo erythema produced either by the sun or by a general application of the arc light.

Four degrees of intensity may be recognized in the skin reactions following therapeutic application of light, as follows:

First Degree. Slight reddening of the skin, which appears a few hours after the application. No itching and burning or peeling of the epidermis.

Second Degree. Pronounced reddening of the skin appearing some hours after the application, accompanied by a moderate degree of smarting or burning or itching and followed after a few days by separation of thin flakes of epidermis.

Third Degree. A very intense reddening of the skin developing several hours after the application. Considerable discomfort, slight swelling and thickening of the skin, but without formation of blisters. After a few days a very pronounced exfoliation similar to that which occurs after scarlet fever.

Fourth Degree. Highly intensive reaction with the formation of vesicles. Intense burning and itching, perhaps accompanied by a slight rise of temperature.

In the employment of the sun bath and general applications of the arc light some practitioners make only first degree applications. Good is without doubt accomplished by applications of this sort, but the opinion is held by most experienced observers that the reactions produced by an application of so little intensity are not sufficiently great to secure the best results even though the applications are renewed every day.

When the application is sufficiently intense to secure an erythema of the second degree, the good results are considerably more pronounced. The general effect of first and second degree applications are tonic and restorative. Such applications tend to encourage a sense of well-being and blood-building.

For the highest degree of efficiency the application should be made of sufficient intensity to produce third degree effects. Such effects, as has been shown by Leonard Hill, develop immunity, as shown by an increase in antibodies in the blood within an hour or two after the application. Reyn, of Copenhagen, systematically aims to produce these third degree effects at the first application. Leonard Hill believes that the best effects may be obtained by producing third degree effects and then allowing an interval of two or three weeks to elapse until the skin recovers its sensitivity, when the application is repeated.

Pigmentation of the Skin

Thus both natural and artificial sunlight cause pigmentation or tanning of the skin. The pigmentation may be produced by repeated light applications or a single intense application. A very pronounced erythema is usually followed by a brown coloration of the skin. The pigment formed is supposed to be derived from tyrosin. Pigmentation is probably related to activity of the suprarenal capsules. Wave lengths of 2,800 A. to 2,900 A. are the most active in producing pigmentation. Pigmentation of the skin following light applications is thought by some to be a defensive process. It is most intense after an erythema dose of moderate intensity.

Rollier aims to produce pigmentation without producing a marked erythema, while Reyn, of Copenhagen, regards the erythema as essential for the best results. In this view he is supported by Leonard Hill. It is well-known that pigmentation occurs most readily and to the most pronounced degree in brunettes. Red-haired, thin-skinned people who freckle easily but who do not tan, are thought to be less likely to benefit greatly from light treatment than do those who tan readily. It is not true, however, that light hair and blue eyes are a contraindication for light treatment or that such persons are not benefited by the use of light baths. The writer has observed little, if any, difference in the beneficial effects of light upon light- and dark-haired persons.

The quartz light produces less pronounced pigmentation than the arc light because the short rays which it produces have little penetrating power, only about 1/250 of an inch, while the longer rays of the arc light have much greater penetrating power and produce pigmentation in the deeper layers of the skin. It is possible, also, that the heating of the skin which occurs in the use of the arc lamp increases the pigmentation.

Pigmentation of the skin does not necessarily prevent erythema. Arning noted that natives of the South Sea Islands living in mountainous regions suffer from solar erythemas notwithstanding the chocolate brown pigmentation of their skins.

That pigmentation of the skin may be produced without either the ultra-violet rays or luminous heat rays is shown by the effect of prolonged applications of moist heat upon the skin. When fomentations are applied daily for several weeks, the skin usually acquires a mottled appearance such as is shown in the accompanying cut. The writer has observed this effect in many scores of cases; in fact, it is the ordinary result of daily repeated and prolonged hot applications, whatever may be the source of heat. Whether this form of pigmentation is identical with that resulting from light applications is perhaps open to question. The distribution of the pigment is certainly different and the pigment seems to be denser and perhaps more deeply seated.

Pigmentation also follows application of mustard plasters and chemical irritants of various sorts.

The tanning of the skin which results from sun baths is much denser and more permanent than that produced by the quartz light. Strahlman and Bernhard note that the pigmentation produced by the arc light, like that due to sunlight, is more intense and durable than that produced by ultra-violet rays alone. The combined effect of the luminous rays and heat rays with ultra-violet light, is evidently much superior to the ultra-violet rays alone.

Bernhard confirms Rollier's observation that "patients who pigment best are cured with the greatest certainty and speed by the sun bath."

Jesimek goes so far as to regard the prognosis bad in cases which do not pigment. He considers the skin pigment of value in the curative process and holds that substances are produced in the skin under the influence of light which produce curative effects when distributed by the blood stream.

Rollier holds that the skin pigment transforms the short rays into longer ones which are then able to penetrate to the deeper tissues and thus produce curative effects in diseased bones and other infected structures. He regards the pigment as a sensitizer, as do also Bernhard and Christian.

Pigmentation as an Indicator

In general, patients who tan readily make rapid progress healthward, and a well-tanned skin may be taken as an evidence that substantial improvement has been made; but Gauvain has called attention to the fact that good pigmentation is not always an indication of progress toward recovery. Such patients may require either a larger or a smaller dose of light treatment, or what is more likely, a modification of some accompanying condition, such as diet, hydriatic applications, etc.

It must be kept constantly in mind that light is not a specific and that its beneficial effects are only due to the reactions of the organism. Simple variation of the intensity of the dosage is sometimes found beneficial. In many cases, an intermission increases the ability of the patient to react favorably. Over-dosage may do much harm, especially to feeble, cachectic patients.

Sensitization of the Skin to Light

The skin's susceptibility to light may be increased in a variety of ways, particularly by the use of fluorescent substances, among the best known of which are hematoporphyrin, erythrosin, and eosin. Quinine and methylene blue are also sensitizers.

When eosin is injected into a frog total paralysis occurs if the frog remains exposed to light, but if kept in the dark no symptoms whatever appear.

The belief was current among the laity more than fifty years ago that malarial chills were sometimes produced by exposure to the sun. It is now known that a general application of ultra-violet light will often produce a chill in persons suffering from chronic malarial infection, probably by encouraging the entrance of the parasites into the general circulation.

In persons suffering from smallpox, pustules do not form in parts which are kept excluded from the light.

The skin may be sensitized to light to such a degree as to produce highly disagreeable effects. In such persons, even a short exposure of the skin to the sunlight or an arc or quartz lamp, may give rise to a very distressing herpetic eruption or "prickly heat."

It is claimed that pigmented moles and warts may become cancerous under the influence of sunlight; however, it is known that cancer is least common in the most sunny countries such as Central Africa, where it is practically unknown, and cases of the spontaneous cure of skin cancer by means of the sun bath have been authoritatively reported.

In sensitized persons, gangrene of the ear lobe or some other part has occurred as the result of exposure to the sun or ultra-violet rays.

Sensitizers may be introduced with the food. Chlorophyl and hematoporphyrin are probably the most common. Other sensitizers are bile, urea, lactic acid, and grape sugar. This is supposed by some authorities to be the cause of "summer rash," a disorder which disappears during the winter months, to reappear in the spring.

Sheep are sometimes sensitized and sickened by Swedish clover. Black sheep are not affected. Horses are in like manner sensitized by mildew and may die of gangrene if exposed to light.

In pellagra, the skin of exposed parts show the effects of sensitization, the cause of which may be moldy food, coupled perhaps with a deficiency of certain vitamins which Bernhard suggests may have for their function to counteract the effect of sensitizers, or regulating their action in the body, for sensitizers may be more or less useful in rendering the body susceptible to light, especially when opportunities for sun-bathing are infrequent.

Histological Changes Induced in the Skin by Light Rays

The histological changes occurring in the normal skin under the influence of light have been studied by Meirowsky, Schmidt and Marcuse, Schiff, Zieler, Stelwagon, Sack, MacLeod, Möller, Unna and others, who agree in general on the following findings:

1. Pronounced dilatation of the superficial and deep cutaneous blood vessels.
2. Migration of the leucocytes.
3. Increase in the number of active tissue cells.
4. Swelling of the collagen.
5. Thickening of the rete mucosum.
6. Hyperplasia of the epidermis and abnormal cornification.
7. Swelling of the prickle cells of the epidermis, due to parenchymatous edema. This swelling is caused by the actinic rays. When the skin is examined microscopically there seem to be small vesicles here and there, due to dilatation of the lymph spaces (MacLeod, Glebowsky).

Meirowsky states that under the stimulus of light, nuclear division of the epithelial cells takes place. Unna claimed that light makes the skin dense and harder, the protoplasm being reduced to keratin.

Glebowsky made a histological study of the process of healing in cases of *lupus* under the influence of light treatment. Twenty-four hours after exposure to light, sections of the skin showed dilatation of the vessels and infiltration of the surrounding parts, with active leucocytes. The tissue spaces were dilated. Small vacuoles were clearly marked in the giant cells. These appearances increased as the number of exposures increased. The giant cells were destroyed entirely on an average after four or five exposures. The degenerative processes in the epithelioid elements were less marked as compared with those in the granulomatous cells where observations show most conclusively the value of light in assisting the tissues in the battle against invading parasites.

The Cosmetic Effect of Light

The change which takes place during the process of pigmentation, is most remarkable. Instead of becoming thicker and harder, as might be expected from exposure in the so-called hardening process, the very opposite change occurs. The pigmented skin becomes thinner, softer, more elastic and altogether finer and more delicate. The black skin of a negro is remarkably fine, soft and silky. Under the process of tanning in the open air, the skin not only becomes delicate and elastic, but loses its wrinkles, acquires an under-padding of fat, and is thus "beautified" in a manner which no cosmetic can equal.

Under the influence of the light bath when systematically applied, the hair and nails grow with increased rapidity. This is especially true in blondes, who have little pigment, from which it may be inferred that the growth of hair is a protective measure. The leaves of the edelweiss and other Alpine flowers are covered with hairs, apparently for protection from the powerful ultra-violet rays of the Alpine sunlight.

A very noticeable effect of pigmentation of the skin is an increased ability to absorb heat. This is very noticeable in the negro, whose skin absorbs heat more quickly but without causing him inconvenience because of the great activity of his sweat glands, by which the surplus heat is quickly removed.

The Effect of Ultra-Violet Rays Upon the Eye

Ultra-violet light from an arc-lamp or quartz lamp, or the intense natural light reflected from snow or ice, produces an intense inflammation of the conjunctiva and is the cause of the snow blindness from which Alpine travelers and mountain climbers sometimes suffer severely. This action of the ultra-violet rays appears to be somewhat akin to the erythema of the skin caused by an intense exposure to the snow or other source of ultra-violet rays, but differing notably in the fact that an attack is not followed by temporary immunity, as in case of the skin.

Recovery from a conjunctivitis, due to ultra-violet rays, usually occurs quickly when the cause of irritation is removed; in this respect differing from conjunctivitis due to infection.

The crystallin lens and other humors of the eye are for some unknown reason not subject to injury by the ultra-violet rays. This was found to be true after exposures so long as 100 hours.

Shackleton records the curious observation that the pigmentation of the eyes as well as that of the skin, was influenced by the absence of light during the Arctic night. The skin became greenish-yellow and brown; and black eyes became blue or grey.

The Skin as an Organ of Defense

The remarkable increase in the immunizing power of the blood demonstrated by Leonard Hill and his associates, suggests that the skin may play an important part in defending the body against infection by raising the immunizing power of the blood under the influence of light rays.

Among civilized people, the skin is universally anemic and enfeebled by the universal practice of over-clothing. In view of the important functions of the skin, there should be a widespread campaign to introduce sun-bathing and the construction of sunny open-air gymnasiums. The tanned skin is able to defend itself against cold and to protect the body against disease much more efficiently than the pale, anemic skin which has not been "kissed by the sun." The importance of the skin functions is impressively illustrated by a tragic incident which occurred in Italy in the 15th century. In preparing picturesque decorations for a feast given by the Duke of Milan, the famous artist Leonardo da Vinci covered a young boy with gold leaf to represent the Golden

Age. The boy became very ill, and every effort was made to remove the gilding but without success, and in a few days, though warmly wrapped, he died in the artist's arms shivering with cold. A warm bath might have saved him.

The dear price we pay for wearing clothes is a great loss in longevity. How much, no one can say, but very likely much more than we would venture to suggest. One of the greatest needs of our modern civilized man is a new skin. And, fortunately, a new, well tanned, disease-resisting skin is available to all who are willing to take the comparatively little trouble required to secure it.

Influence of Heat on Light Effects

The effects of light upon the skin are very notably influenced by temperature. For example, Leonard Hill showed that in a room of ordinary temperature (70° F.) the mercury-vapor lamp placed at a distance of 10 inches from the skin produced an erythema in ten minutes, while under the same conditions in a cold room an exposure of one hour was required to produce the same amount of reaction. The application of hot water to the skin greatly increases its sensitiveness to ultra-violet rays, whereas the application of cold water produces the opposite effect.

More than 30 years ago the writer observed that by directing a current of air upon the skin during an application of light from an arc lamp, much higher intensities of light could be employed and the application could be considerably prolonged without producing excessive irritation of the skin. This plan was adopted and has been since used in the author's practice with the idea that by thus protecting the surface much larger quantities of light rays might be made to reach the deeper tissues, thus increasing the therapeutic effects desired.

It was observed by Sobotka that anything which produces redness or active hyperemia of the skin will increase the effect of the ultra-violet rays. A passive hyperemia, however, as shown by a bluish tint of the skin, has no effect.

The observation of Sobotka, which any clinical observer may easily verify, shows the superiority of the arc lamp over the mercury arc or quartz lamp as a source of light for general therapeutic use.

Keller showed that mustard plasters produce a much less pronounced effect upon the skin when light applications have previously been made. The same is true of other irritants. After light treatment the skin is less subject to boils, acne and other skin infections. X-ray experts have noted that light applications to the skin enable it to receive stronger doses of the X-ray without injury.

The Influence of Light Upon the Cutaneous Glands

Exposure to intense light rays causes profuse perspiration. It is not necessary that the atmosphere in contact with the body should be of a high temperature; in fact, the temperature of the air about the body may be considerably below the normal body temperature. The stimulation of the perspiratory glands by the light rays excites their activity to a remarkable degree. The writer observed this in his early experiments with the electric-light bath in 1891, and later, in 1894, reported a series of experiments which showed that the amount of perspiration produced in the electric-light bath as compared with that produced in the Turkish bath was nearly double, while the time which elapsed before the appearance of perspiration was very much less in the light bath than in the Turkish bath. Professor Winternitz, of Vienna, mentioned to the writer in 1899 an observation of considerable interest in this connection. In the use of the writer's electric-light bath, which he had installed both in the Polyclinic connected with the medical department of the university and in his own medical establishment at Kaltenleutgeben, he constantly observed that perspiration began sooner on the outer portions of the thighs which were more directly exposed to the influence of the light rays than upon the inner surfaces. He also observed active perspiration in an atmosphere at a temperature much below that of the body, and in one case at a temperature as low as 65° F., in a neurasthenic patient who was particularly susceptible to the stimulus of radiant energy. A much higher temperature than this is required in the vapor bath, the hot-air bath or the Turkish bath, showing that the effect produced must be due to the stimulation of the sweat glands by the light rays.

Many years ago the writer had an odd experience in riding up Pikes Peak, late in the season, in one of the old-fashioned coaches in use at that time. Sitting upon the sunny side of the covered coach, one ear was in the sunshine, the other in the shadow. The ear in the shadow was frozen stiff in the frosty Alpine air and was severely frost-bitten, while the other ear though perfectly comfortable, at the time, was the next morning greatly swollen and most uncomfortable with sunburn.

The Influence of Light Upon General Metabolism

The following is quoted from the writer's chapter on Heliotherapy, in volume IX of *The International System of Physiologic Therapeutics:*

"An animal eliminates more carbon dioxid under the influence of light than when confined in the dark. This has been found to be true of hibernating animals also. Starving animals lose less weight at night than during an equal number of hours of daylight, although kept equally quiet. Certain animals, as crabs, when painted with dark varnish, are quickly killed, although unaffected by transparent varnish (Heile).

"Eggs develop more rapidly when exposed to the influence of sunlight than when kept in the dark. This is also true of the larvæ of insects.

"Metabolism is unquestionably stimulated by the reflex action set up by the light rays impinging upon the nerve-endings of the skin and retina. Oxidation of living tissues is increased by the action of sunlight (Quincke), while in human beings, as well as in animals, less carbon-dioxid is eliminated at night than during the same number of hours of daylight, even though an equal degree of quiet be observed (Pettenkofer and Voit). Country children, who are more exposed to sunshine than those in the city, are much healthier in appearance and less subject to rickets, tuberculosis and other grave disorders. Cretinism is most frequently found in deep valleys from which the direct rays of the sun are largely excluded. Eskimo women suffer from amenorrhea during the long polar night."

The oyster closes his shell when placed in the dark.

Hess, Steenbock and others have proven that calcium metabolism is profoundly influenced by light. Deprived of light, babies and experimental animals suffer from rachitis. The bones remain soft and undergo changes due to deficient assimilation of lime. Bony fishes that live in the depths of the ocean have cartilaginous skeletons, apparently because they are deprived of light.

In the Mississippi valley and some other parts of the United States, where the sky is much clouded, rickets occurs in a large proportion of the population. The natives of Central Africa are wholly free from the disease. In the Sahara Desert, among the Bedouins and natives of the Aures Mountains, the writer looked in vain for a case of rickets.

Effects of Light Upon the Blood Vessels

Those portions of the skin which are habitually exposed to light have a much more active circulation than those parts of the skin which are covered. They are also better prepared to protect themselves against changes of temperature and show a higher degree of resistance generally. The color of skin surfaces which are habitually exposed to light is not only darker but ruddier because of the increased circulation of blood through the part. Blood vessels of such parts are more widely dilated and more numerous than in parts protected from the action of light. When an exposure to light is of such a character as to produce erythema, the most intense cutaneous congestion results, such as might be induced by the application of mustard, a fomentation or by chemical, thermal or mechanical irritants of other sorts. The congestion produced by the chemical ray differs, however, from that induced by a fomentation in that it is remarkably lasting. One observer reports, as the result of experiments upon himself, that the increased vascularity resulting from a solar erythema was still noticeable six months later. This property of the ultra-violet ray is of great value in therapeutics, as it affords a most admirable method of producing derivative effects with which may be combated pain, congestions and inflammations in deep-lying parts. It is often in the highest degree important that such effects be secured as the best means of affording definite relief in cases of visceral congestion of various sorts, particularly in such disorders as chronic bronchitis, gastritis, hepatic congestion, intestinal catarrh, ovarian and other pelvic congestions, congestion of the spinal cord, etc. The writer has for years made use of various phototherapeutic appliances for securing these effects and with most excellent results, and believes that he was the first to point out and apply this use of solar and electric light.

Sonne has shown that the blood vessels are affected chiefly by the penetrating, luminous heat waves rather than by the ultraviolet rays.

Bernhard notes that the lymph circulation is accelerated by light treatment as well as the blood movement.

Hasselbach noted that the increased vascularity of the skin induced by light treatment lasts for six to nine months.

Marked lowering of blood pressure after irradiation with an arc light has been demonstrated by Reed, Hasselbach and others.

Kimmerle noted that the effect of the arc lamp in lowering blood pressure was more marked than that of the quartz lamp, doubtless because of the effects upon the cutaneous vessels induced by the penetrating luminous and inner red rays of the arc light.

The Influence of Light Upon the Blood

Under the influence of general light applications in anemic persons the red blood cells increase in number, the hemoglobin increases proportionately and the red cells produced are more highly resistant and longer lived. There is also an increase in the number of white blood cells. There is a decrease in blood sugar and of tyrosin and an increase of calcium, phosphorus and agglutinins.

The increase of leucocytes occurs within half an hour after a general light application and may amount to as much as 90 per cent. (Traugott). The average increase is 25 to 30 per cent.

There is a marked increase in immunity. This may result from a single exposure and even before the appearance of pigment occurs (Hill).

Within an hour or two after a general light bath of sufficient intensity to produce a decided erythema, the bactericidal power of the blood is notably increased. This shows that exposure of the skin to light increases the power to resist disease. Experiments with rabbits have shown that continuous exposure even to feeble sources of ultra-violet light has the effect to protect them against inoculation with cancer. This experiment is highly important since it suggests the possibility that lack of sunshine may be one of the causes of the great prevalence and rapid increase of cancer among civilized people. It also suggests the importance of employing sunshine, natural and artificial, as a preventive of cancer. Persons who have been subjected to operations or other treatment for cancer should take care to have their skins thoroughly tanned and keep them tanned by applications of natural or artificial sunlight. Sunlight should also be employed as a preventive measure in all cases in which there is a hereditary predisposition to cancer.

Light increases the hemoglobin of the red cells. Hemoglobin absorbs light to a considerable degree and in a peculiar manner, as shown by the characteristic absorption bands of the spectrum.

Hertel holds the view that light rays cause a splitting off of oxygen from the plasma of the blood and tissues much in the same way as oxygen is set free from plants under the influence of light. He believes that this process affects both animal tissues and bacteria. Quincke demonstrated that under the influence of light the hemoglobin gives off its oxygen more quickly than in the dark. He regards this as a proof that light increases the oxidizing power of the blood, and that thereby the process of oxidation in the human body may be encouraged.

Graffenberger claims to have proved that the hemoglobin content of the red cells is diminished in the absence of light, and that prolonged darkness causes a lessening of the total quantity of the blood. Marti showed that in rats absence of light diminishes the number of red cells and the amount of hemoglobin. Strong continuous light accelerates the formation of red blood cells and also the amount of the hemoglobin content. Although Borrisow was not able to confirm this observation, he found in his experiments that dogs kept in the light, after a brief decline, gained in weight considerably, and that appetite was increased, while dogs left in darkness showed no gain in weight. According to Freund the oxyhemoglobin bands in persons examined at the close of the polar night showed signs of extension.

Finsen enveloped the body of a tadpole in moistened filter paper, and after attaching it in proper position to the stage of a miscroscope, exposed it to the rays of the sun. During the exposure the miscroscopic examination showed dilatation of the capillaries, slowing of the blood-stream and migration of the white cells, phenomena which are usually observed in simple inflammation. The red cells contracted. Uskoff found that the white cells of frog's blood showed more and longer processes in red than in violet light. In red light they were spread out in the form of thin, hardly visible discs. Hermann claims that the leucocytes are not sensitive to light, but that the red cells usually change their shape.

Axmann found that venous blood after long exposure to the air turns a bright red when exposed to the ultra-violet rays. He believes this effect is due to the nascent ozone. He remarks that fresh and suppurating wounds behaved under the influence of the actinic rays as if they had been swabbed with hydrogen peroxide.

Penetrating, luminous heat rays act not only upon the connective tissue, muscular and nerve cells with which they come in contact, but also upon the red and white blood-cells circulating in the vessels. As these short heat rays are able to penetrate to a depth of two inches or more, it is evident that the blood circulating through the larger arterial and venous trunks is brought under their influence as well as the blood-cells moving through the smaller vessels. Through its rapid movement through the blood vessels, the entire volume of blood in the body may be thus exposed to the stimulating influence of thermic rays within a comparatively short time. As a result, the functional activities of both the white and red cells may be greatly stimulated. The oxidation of waste matters will thus be greatly increased, while the destruction by phagocytes of bacteria and debris resulting from accident or by disease will be greatly stimulated.

Nerve pressure and pain are relieved by exciting the activity of the circulation in areas which are the seat of passive congestion.

Schläpfer claims to have demonstrated that the blood takes up electro-magnetic energy when irradiated and distributes it to the various organs.

Riedel declares that an increase of skin pigment indicates an increase of hemoglobin.

The Influence of Light Upon the Nervous System

Very strong light often produces giddiness, headache, and sometimes nausea, as the result of overstimulation of the optic nerve, doubtless through reflex action. Exposure of the head to the direct rays of the sun, and sometimes even exposure of the general skin surface, produces the same and often even more intense effects. Sunstroke affords an illustration of the powerful influence of the chemical rays upon the nervous system, the evil effects of the sun's rays manifested in this condition being due not to heat but rather to the chemical elements of the sun's rays. When traveling in Egypt, the writer often observed natives plodding along the road in the middle of the day with their bodies almost entirely nude, but with a large shawl or scarf coiled about their heads in a huge mass for protection against the intense action of the sunlight. The black wooly hair of the negro and his thick scalp and skull afford the best possible protection against the pernicious influence of the sun's rays upon the brain. Biology teaches us that the eye is simply a modification of the skin. The optic nerve is especially sensitive to the luminous rays of light, while the cutaneous nerves, certain of them at least, are especially susceptible to the chemical rays. Through the influence of these rays upon the skin, strong excitant or tonic impressions are being constantly made upon the central nervous system, modifying all the nutritive processes and aiding in the maintenance of efficient activity in every vital organ.

The effect of ultra-violet light in producing resistance to fatigue is very marked. The subject is more alert mentally as well as physically. The beneficial effects upon the nervous system appear to be produced by the influence of light upon the sympathetic system (Saidman).

The mind is notably influenced by light. Said Müller, "We are never witty in the dark."

Helmholtz, one of the greatest thinkers of the last century and who spent much of his life in researches pertaining to light, noted that new and brilliant ideas "came with special facility"—"in sunny weather," and "never enter a tired brain."

Many observers have noted that children exposed to light in open-air schools make better progress than those kept indoors.

Rikli believed that light is a food, supplying to the nervous system some subtle element which it requires. The recent observations of Steenbock, of Wisconsin University, and his associates have convincingly shown that ultra-violet light rays may actually replace a certain element of the food, the vitamin D which prevents rickets.

Light and Reproduction

Hill has suggested that the loss of breeding power in man and animals may be due to lack of sunshine. There are several established facts which bear out this view. Chickens lay more eggs and cows give more milk when exposed to air and sunlight. The Eskimo women cease to menstruate during the long winter night. The falling birth rate in all civilized countries suggests the necessity for a world-wide campaign of education concerning the value of sunlight. The whole world needs more light.

THE PHYSIOLOGIC EFFECTS OF VISIBLE AND INFRA-RED HEAT RAYS

Up to the present time, in their studies of the physiologic effects of light, physicists and physiologists have confined themselves almost exclusively to observations upon the influence of the ultra-violet rays. It is quite natural that this should be the case for the reason that the erythema, tanning and other effects of the ultra-violet rays, are highly unique and striking; while the effects of the visible rays, especially the red, and of the invisible infra-red rays, are much more subtle, and on superficial examination, appear to be not essentially different from the familiar heat effects produced by ordinary contacts with warm water, hot air and other heated objects.

But science has clearly demonstrated that there is a decided difference between the heat effects produced by mere contact with non-luminous, heated objects and those produced by irradiation from luminous bodies.

These effects differ both in kind and quantitatively. Radiant heat produces all the effects obtainable from non-radiant heat sources and important, additional effects; consequently, in the study of the physiologic effects of infra-red rays, it is necessary to study the effects of heat in general.

Discovery of the Therapeutic Value of Radiant Heat

My own attention was accidentally called to the remarkable penetrating property of the red rays, many years ago (1891). In turning the switch of an incandescent lamp, I noticed, as my hand happened to pass between the lamp and my eyes, a red glow of the fingers, especially distinct at the nails and joints. In the case of the little finger, the entire finger glowed with a deep red light. This led me to experiment.

I found when a small incandescent lamp was placed in the mouth, the cheeks glowed; and when a similar lamp was placed in the vagina of a patient with little abdominal fat, a red glow appeared, in a darkened room, over a circular area extending nearly from the pubis to the umbilicus. I recognized at once that I was in the possession of a new, highly useful, therapeutic agent.

Previous experiments had shown me that the heat from heated bodies placed in contact with the skin, even very intense, could be made to penetrate only a very short distance, because the heat was carried away by the constantly moving blood and lymph as rapidly as it was transmitted by conduction to the deeper layers of the skin and underlying tissues.

Here was a form of heat which, as radiant energy, would penetrate instantly into the depths of the tissues to the extent of at least two inches or more, as my experiments showed. I was considerably excited over the discovery of this new and precious resource which might prove of immense value as a therapeutic means for the relief of pain and as a means of applying thermic stimulation to the subdermic structures. I proceeded at once to construct cabinets and appliances of various sorts for utilizing radiant heat, and have since that time made continuous and extensive use of both the incandescent light and the arc light in thermic applications, both local and general.

I also began, with the aid of my students, a series of experiments for the purpose of determining the physiologic effects of the electric-light bath. Some of the observations made were detailed in a paper read by the writer before the American Electro-Therapeutic Association at its fourth annual meeting, New York, September 25, 1894. An account was given of the physiologic effects of the electric-light cabinet bath, the effects of which are essentially those of the infra-red rays, from which the following is quoted:

The Physiologic Effects of the Electric-Light Bath

"My earliest experiments in the use of the electric-light bath showed me that it was capable of producing very characteristic effects. This led me to undertake a series of physiologic experiments for the purpose of placing its therapeutic use upon a rational basis, and for the purpose of comparing the effects of the electric-light, Turkish, and Russian baths. The objects of the experiments were to determine the effects of the electric-light bath as compared with those of the Turkish and the Russian baths upon—

"1. CO_2 elimination.

"2. Urinary secretion.

"3. Perspiration.

"4. Surface and internal temperature.

"5. The number of blood corpuscles and the amount of hemoglobin.

"The results of these experiments and the methods employed may be summarized as follows:

"1. **CO_2 Elimination.**—Three healthy young men were subjected to the influence of the incandescent electric light or radiant heat bath for five, ten, twenty, and thirty minutes, respectively, the time being the same for each, and all other conditions being made as nearly alike as possible. The same young men were likewise subjected to the influence of the Turkish and the Russian baths for the same lengths of time, but on different days, care being taken to maintain a uniform dietary during the entire series of experiments, at the same hours of the day. The influence of the bath upon CO_2 elimination was determined by carefully measuring with a delicate air meter which I had constructed for the purpose, all the air expired during the ten minutes before the experiment, collecting an average sample of the air for analysis. During the bath the air was collected for the same length of time. In a case in which the bath lasted only five minutes, the figures were doubled so as to make them comparable with the rest. In case the bath lasted twenty minutes or more, the air was measured and collected during the last ten minutes; the results obtained were corrected for barometric pressure and vapor tension so that the figures given in the table for the different experiments are, in every respect, properly comparable. The results were as follows:

"The average per cent of CO_2 obtained before the experiment was 3.60.

"For the electric-light bath the averages per cent obtained were as follows:

5 minutes	4.10	20 minutes	4.20
10 minutes	4.10	30 minutes	5.10 and 5.13

"In a repetition of the thirty-minute bath, the higher percentage of 5.13 was obtained.

"For the Turkish bath the averages per cent obtained were:

5 minutes	4.03	10 minutes	4.07
	30 minutes	4.01	

"For the Russian bath the per cent was 3.96 for a bath of thirty minutes.

"The highest amount of CO_2 elimination was 4.29 litres, which was in the incandescent electric light bath for thirty minutes.

"The temperature of the air in the baths was as follows:

"Electric-light bath, 28 to 36° C. (85 to 97° F.), or constantly below the temperature of the body; Russian bath, 38° C. (100° F.); Turkish bath, 55° C. (131-155° F.).

"2. Urinary Secretion.—The following table shows the average figures obtained from the three young men who were the subjects of experiment. The facts determined in relation to the urine were: the amount, the specific gravity, the acidity, the amount of urea, the amount of uric acid, the total chlorides expressed in terms of HCl, the phosphoric acid, and the total solids. The figures given were determined by accurate quantitative analysis of the whole amount secreted in twenty-four hours. The figures obtained in relation to the most important of these quantities were as follows:

Electric-light bath: urea............................26.32 gms.
    Total chlorides .... 5.25 "
    Total solids ....49.30 "
Turkish bath: urea................................27.39 "
    Total chlorides .... 6.91 "
    Total solids ....52.70 "
Russian bath: urea................................29.56 "
    Total chlorides .... 7.60 "
    Total solids ....55.14 "

"The figures obtained for the urine were the exact reverse of those obtained for the CO_2 elimination.

"The diminished amount of urea, total chlorides, and total solids present in the urine during the twenty-four hours in which the subject was subjected to the electric-light bath, was evidently the result of increased elimination by the skin, showing that the electric-light bath is much more powerful than either the Turkish or the Russian bath as a means of stimulating vicarious eliminative work upon the part of the skin.

"The amount of perspiration induced by the incandescent electric-light bath was fully double that induced by the Turkish bath in the same length of time.

"The amount of perspiration induced by the Russian bath was less than that induced by the electric-light and the Turkish bath.

"3. **Perspiration.**—Two points were determined in reference to perspiration:

(1) The time required to induce perspiration.

(2) The temperature at which perspiration began.

"The averages were as follows:

"**Incandescent Electric-Light Bath:** Time required to induce perspiration, three minutes, thirty-two seconds. The average temperature of the cabinet at which perspiration appeared was 27.2 degrees C. (81 degrees F.).

"**Turkish Bath:** The time required to induce perspiration, five minutes, thirty-five seconds. Temperature of the bath, 53.6 degrees C. (128.5 degrees F.).

"**Russian Bath:** The time required for perspiration, six minutes, forty-five seconds. Temperature, 101.8 degrees F.

"The above figures show very clearly the superior value of the electric-light bath as a means of stimulating cutaneous activity.

"4. **Surface and Internal Temperature.**—The influence of the bath upon surface and internal temperature is a matter of importance, since Bouchard has shown that the heat-regulating apparatus of the body is called into operation by a rise in the temperature of the blood equal to .40° C. (.72° F.).

"In experiments made in December, 1891, for the purpose of determining the effect of the bath upon surface and internal temperature, I obtained the following results in a comparative study of the effects of the electric bath and the Turkish bath upon surface and internal temperature:

"**Electric-Light Bath:** Temperature of bath, 34.5° C. (94° F.); internal temperature of subject before the bath, 36.6° C. (97.9° F.); surface temperature, 35° C. (95° F.) Patient began to perspire after one minute. At the end of five and a half minutes he was removed from the bath. The temperature was taken at once and the internal temperature was found to be 37.5° C. (99.6° F.); the surface temperature, 37.9° C. (100.2° F.). Ten minutes after the bath the mouth temperature was 37° C. (98.5° F.); the axillary temperature was 36.6° C. (98° F.).

"**Turkish Bath:** Temperature of bath, 70.5° C. (159° F.). Temperature of the subject before the bath, 36.4° C. (97.4° F.); axillary temperature, 96° F. Perspiration began in five and a half minutes. Immediately after the bath, the mouth temperature was found to be 37° C. (98.7° F.); axillary temperature, 37.2° C. (99° F.). Ten minutes later the mouth temperature was 37° C. (98.8° F.); axillary temperature, 36.6° C. (98° F.).

"From these statements it appears that the incandescent electric-light bath is far more effective than the Turkish bath in raising both surface and internal temperature, which clearly indicates the penetrative power of the intense heat rays of the electric light.

"5. **The Blood.**—The immediate effects of the incandescent electric-light bath upon the blood were determined by a careful count of the corpuscles by Gower's instruments and a determination of the hemoglobin by the hematoscope of Henocque. The figures obtained showed no very marked increase in either blood corpuscles or hemoglobin, although in one case the number of corpuscles was increased nearly 200,000 per cubic millimeter.

"The physiological effects of the incandescent electric-light bath are chiefly those of heat, and do not differ very essentially from the effects obtained from other sources of heat, except that the electric-light bath is a much more efficient and convenient method of administering heat than any other which has been devised, with the exception of water."*

Observations of Winternitz

These observations were later fully confirmed by Winternitz, of Vienna, who referred to the bath as follows:

"The electric-light bath presents an advantage over every other means of applying heat in the readiness with which the dosage may be regulated as regards time and intensity. The instant the switch controlling the circuit is closed the whole force of the bath or that portion of it in use is brought to bear at once upon the body. The instant the circuit is opened the heat is wholly and absolutely withdrawn. By means of properly adjusted switches, whereby the number of lamps in use may be controlled, the amount of heat applied may be exactly regulated.

"Another advantage of the electric-light bath is that it does not interfere with heat elimination. It, in fact, encourages heat elimination by encouraging free perspiration. Many other forms of hot applications, particularly hot-water baths and sweating packs, cause retention of bodily heat. In the electric-light bath, the heat elimination and the excretion of effete matters which accompany vigorous perspiration, proceed with increased activity at the same time the rays of radiant heat are penetrating the tissues, elevating the temperature of the blood, and quickening vital processes.

"The importance of this property of the electric-light bath is clearly shown by the interesting experiments of Conrad Klar. This investigator showed by calorimetric experiment that with the body exposed in an atmosphere somewhat below the body temperature, heat elimination was during the first five minutes ten

---

* "The Incandescent Electric-Light or Radiant Heat Bath," New York, 1894.

times the normal amount: while during the second five minutes the amount of heat eliminated was half as great. The diminished loss during the second five minutes was doubtless due to contraction of the blood vessels of the skin. In the electric-light bath the cutaneous vessels are thoroughly relaxed, and this condition is maintained by the action of the rays of light falling upon the skin while the air about the patient is but little above the ordinary atmospheric temperature, a condition which in the highest degree favors heat elimination.

"The electric-light bath is a new invention by Kellogg, Battle Creek, Mich., U. S. A. It is undoubtedly true that radiant heat penetrates the tissues much better than conducted heat, and it is very probable also that the inner life of the cell is influenced by the radiant heat, either qualitatively or quantitatively, and to a higher degree. All the effects of the vapor bath can be produced by the electric-light bath. The loss of carbonic acid gas is considerably greater in the electric-light bath than in the vapor bath, and what is especially remarkable, perspiration occurs very quickly and at a very low temperature, and is very profuse. [Indications of perspiration are sometimes noticed at 28° C. (95° F.). The author has observed perspiration at 85° F., and Professor Winternitz stated to him personally (1899) that he had seen moisture appear upon the skin in a single instance at 65° F. The patient was a somewhat excitable neurasthenic, and very susceptible to the stimulus of radiant energy.]

"Ordinarily a much higher temperature is necessary before symptoms of sweating occur in the vapor bath. The time required to produce sweating in the electric-light bath is commonly 3½ minutes, whereas about five minutes are required in the vapor bath. Finally the quantity of perspiration is considerably greater in the electric-light bath. That the radiant heat is the main cause of this, and not the heated air, was evident from the observations made by us that the external part of the leg upon which the rays of light directly fell perspired very much more quickly and profusely than the internal part of the leg, which received only reflected rays. After 10 to 30 minutes the body temperature increased to 40° C. (104° F.). the pulse to 160. respiration to 42.—

symptoms of the condition resembling fever. We have used the electric-light bath in ways analogous to the use of the vapor bath in a number of cases of sclerosis, rheumatism, and gout, and have been much gratified with the results. We have as yet made no further experiments. Kellogg reports very good results in sclerosis, arthritis, and many disorders of nutrition. Lehmann has been very successful in psoriasis. Since we have in the electric-light bath a thermal method by which the degree of heat applied can be exactly measured and regulated, and knowing the powerful influence of light upon the life of the cell and of the whole organism, we believe that this method will hold a prominent place among the forms of thermal applications, and that we shall be enabled by its use to influence a series of maladies more quickly, more effectively, and more satisfactorily than heretofore."

A striking proof of the superior penetrating power of the luminous red rays was given by Rubner many years ago (1894). This careful observer noted that for a given length of time and a given area a far greater amount of heat may be introduced into the tissues through the skin in the employment of sunlight than when heat from such a source as an Argand burner is employed. He found, for example, that heat from an Argand burner allowed to fall upon the forehead was unendurable when the intensity of the heat reached 0.3 calory per minute, whereas an intensity of 1.0 calory per minute gave no inconvenience when the source of heat was the sun's rays.

The reason for this is to be found in the fact that in the case of sunlight the luminous heat rays constitute nearly one-third of the total energy, whereas in the flame of an Argand burner the luminous rays constitute only about 3 per cent. of the total energy, the balance consisting of infra-red rays. This experiment shows very clearly the very pronounced difference in penetrating power between luminous heat rays and infra-red rays.

Heated bodies, metal for example, become incandescent, or red hot, at a temperature a little below 1,000° F. Below this temperature only invisible, or infra-red rays, are emitted. As the temperature rises, visible and ultra-violet rays are given off. At the same time the volume of infra-red rays increases although the proportion of visible and ultra-violet rays to infra-red rays increases as the temperature rises.

Carl Sonne, of Copenhagen, the able physicist associated with the Finsen Institute, has recently made a careful study of this question, the results of which he has presented in a series of papers from which through his courtesy we are permitted to abstract and quote as follows:

Although sunlight is very rich in luminous rays because of its high temperature, two-thirds of its energy still consists of infra-red rays. The infra-red rays of the carbon arc light constitute about four-fifths of its total radiant energy, the proportion of infra-red rays decreasing as the amperage is increased. For each additional ampere of current used an arc light yields 300 to 400 additional candle power. Infra-red rays constitute about 53 per cent of the quartz light.

Sonne thinks it necessary to distinguish between the effects of the two kinds of infra-red rays, the inner and the outer rays. The outer infra-red rays are the rays of longer wave length at the far end of the spectrum, while the inner infra-red rays are the rays of shorter wave length which lie next to the visible spectrum just below the red, having wave lengths of 8,000 A. or longer.

The rays thrown off by ordinary heated bodies such as hot stoves and most terrestrial sources of light are chiefly outer infra-red rays. In the case of the arc light, the temperature being higher, the chief output of energy is in the inner infra-red region, and in the case of sunlight in the luminous region of the spectrum. Says Sonne, "It is only the sunlight and the carbon arc light which contain any large quantities of infra-red rays. The outer infra-red rays, that is, the longer rays, *have a very low power of penetration.*" It is for this reason that the finest screen of water or glass is sufficient protection from the radiant heat of a stove. The penetrating power of the inner infra-red rays is, however, much higher, a fact easily demonstrated with an open fire.

Sonne found that the flexor side of the forearm tolerated per square centimeter a radiation per minute of 3.11 calories of visible rays, 1.79 calories inner infra-red rays, 1.35 outer infra-red rays.

The temperatures employed were in all cases as high as could be endured without burning.

The figures found by Sonne are considerably higher than those of Rubner, which Sonne explains as being due to the fact that Rubner "did not go so far as to determine the extreme point at which destruction of the skin could just be avoided, but chiefly aimed at ascertaining when, for instance, the radiant heat from a reading lamp became unendurably troublesome, which is of course long before the radiant heat will cause combustion."

This experiment clearly demonstrates the superior penetrating power of the luminous heat rays and shows that even the inner infra-red rays have little more than half the penetrating power of the luminous heat rays and that their penetrating power diminishes as the wave length increases. The conclusion reached by Sonne was that the penetrating power of the visible heat rays is practically double that of the infra-red. On testing the temperature of the skin he found the surface temperature to be after radiation with visible rays 3.1° F. lower than after radiation with outer infra-red rays; but on taking the temperature of the skin 15 seconds after the conclusion of the radiation, the figures were reversed, the temperature of the skin after radiation with visible rays being 1.8° F. higher than after radiation with infra-red rays. The evident explanation is that the visible heat rays penetrated the tissues more deeply than did the infra-red rays so that the amount of heat accumulated was greater and a longer time was required for its dissipation.

We quote as follows from an abstract by Carl Sonne, of Copenhagen, of his several valuable papers presenting a thorough and comprehensive study of this question:

"During infra-red radiation the temperature falls gradually from the surface temperature of 45.5° C. (113.9° F.), until at the depth of 1 cm. the temperature becomes stable at 37° C. (98.6° F.).

"On exposure to luminous rays a rise of temperature occurs from the surface inward, reaching a maximum at a depth of 0.5 cm., where a temperature of 47.5° C. (117.5° F.) is reached. Under infra-red radiation the temperature at the same depth is 41.7° C. (107.1° F.) or 5.8° C. (10.4° F.) lower.

"By radiating the skin surface with luminous rays we are thus able to heat the blood in and beneath the skin to a temperature that is several degrees (5.8° C.) [10.4° F.] higher than the temperature obtained during a radiation of maximum intensity with infra-red rays.

"Therapeutic effects may be thus expected from the visible heat rays.

"The luminous rays have a specific power to heat the blood in and beneath the skin for the reason that the chief absorption of luminous rays does not occur until the rays reach the sanguiferous layers. The luminous rays pass fairly unimpaired through the superficial layers of the skin. The infra-red rays, on the other hand, are almost immediately absorbed in the superficial layers of the skin. These layers are consequently quickly heated, giving rise to a sensation of pain with a comparatively low amount of radiant energy. On this account, the amount of energy which may be absorbed is far greater in the case of luminous rays than with ordinary dark or infra-red heat rays. The energy radiated by luminous rays produces effects both locally upon the skin and upon the general temperature wholly different from those produced by the most intense endurable radiation with infra-red rays.

"In a general light bath about half the body is exposed to a radiation approaching the maximum intensity that can be endured without injury. Thus, enormous volumes of radiant energy are absorbed. In a successful general light bath the body temperature is not allowed to rise to any great extent. When the temperature rises to fever level the patient feels unwell and the bath should be interrupted. The body eliminates the surplus heat by means of sweat and heat elimination from the non-radiated surface. By means of luminous heat rays a considerable portion of the body tissues and the contained blood may be heated to a temperature exceeding fever temperature but without causing an appreciable rise in the general temperature, thus averting injury.

"The question which now presents itself is, therefore, Is there any reason for supposing that this specific heating of the blood in and below the skin surface by means of luminous rays can be of any value to the body as a curative in the case of disease? Several authors have shown that raising the body temperature of animals produces increased tolerance toward various infections. It has been demonstrated that heating the body has an effect upon the formation of antibodies. Rabbits whose blood serum had been made hemolytic by intravenous injection of sheep's blood, were found to have the hemolytic capacity increased by immersing the animals in hot water, whereas the opposite effect was produced by cooling the animals. While heat from fever often produces highly deleterious and destructive effects, even endangering life when a certain level is exceeded, luminous heat has an opposite effect. A general light bath will raise the temperature of the body and thereby produce beneficial effects with no harmful effects.

"Quincke's experiments showed that oxidation is much increased by heating the blood.

"Langley showed that the solar-constant, that is, the amount of heat radiated by the sun upon one cubic centimeter per minute, before reaching the earth's atmosphere, is about 3.0 calories, while the amount of heat emanated by the sun at sea level for the same time and area seldom exceeds 1.0 calory.

"The greatest loss of light passing through the atmosphere is in the ultra-violet and luminous· rays. The invisible rays [infrared] reach the surface of the earth almost unimpaired. Most of the loss of the energy of the sunlight occurs in the lower layers of the atmosphere. The mountain sun is thus richer in both ultra-violet rays and luminous rays and consequently has greater heating power. The temperature of the mountain air is lower. The temperature falls 0.63° C. (1.1° F.) for each 100 meters increased altitude.

"Experiments with guinea-pigs showed that radiation with invisible rays caused no elevation of body temperature, but the body temperature was raised by luminous rays. This may assist us in understanding the significance of pigmentation in Rollier's method of treatment. If the skin is blackened and afterwards exposed to visible rays exclusively, it is found that much less radiant energy will be tolerated than before the blackening.

"I can endure a radiation of light of an intensity of about 85° C. measured on a ray thermometer when the skin is clean. The same skin when blackened by smoke will only endure the same rays at an intensity of 60° measured with the ray thermometer. The reason for this is of course that the luminous rays are to a great extent absorbed by the dark color from whence it reacts partly as conductive heat and partly as invisible heat rays. In the same way we may imagine pigmentation from the sunlight to act. It transforms some of the luminous rays in the mountain sunlight to dark rays, thereby preventing a too vigorous heating of the blood through the absorption of luminous rays. According to this it will be readily understood that Rollier must proceed with the utmost care when a patient is initially subjected to sun baths and that vigorous pigmentation is of such great significance for the patient. In beginning, only small portions of the body surface should be exposed to the light and for a short period only, slowly proceeding under constant measurements of the temperature, and only in those cases where a fine and vigorous pigmentation is obtained will the organism be able to regulate the heat so as to endure the prolonged solar radiation to which it may be most profitably exposed in order to obtain beneficial results.

Relative value of the luminous heat rays of the arc light and of sunlight as compared with the infra-red or non-visible heat rays.

"Quite differently in the case of the carbon arc light. It contains fewer luminous rays and a far larger amount of dark infra-red rays than the sunlight. The risk for the human organism of receiving more absorption of luminous heat in the blood than can be tolerated is very slight, so pigmentation of the skin is not needed as in the case of the sunlight bath. Besides, the intense infra-red heat from the lamps will also prevent the subject from getting so near to the lamp as to absorb too much heat. If, however, this risk should be incurred, the infra-red heat will help to produce an abundant perspiration by which the infra-red heat will be absorbed, thus making it possible to approach nearer to the lamp and so obtain an intense light radiation.

Summary

"The current view that the therapeutic effect of the general light bath should be essentially due to the ultra-violet rays has not been demonstrated.

"Based on a series of facts concerning the specific absorption relations of visible heat rays during radiation to the human skin, the following theory is advanced:

"The curative effect of the general light bath is due to the capacity of the luminous rays during the light bath to heat a very essential portion of the blood volume of the organism to a temperature exceeding that of fever temperature without causing the body temperature to rise to any appreciable degree."

Since it is known that light rays only become useful when absorbed, the novel views presented by Sonne in the above paragraphs appeal to the writer as offering a most reasonable rationale of the physiologic and therapeutic effects of light. The experimental work done by myself and my students in 1893-4 studied exclusively the thermic effects of the visible and infra-red rays. In the first edition of this work (1910) special emphasis was laid upon the thermic effects produced by both the incandescent light cabinet and the arc light. Most authors who attribute to the ultra-violet rays exclusively the effects of sunlight and artificial light greatly limit the scope of light as a therapeutic agent and fall far short of appreciating its full value as a curative means.

Light Therapy

The curative properties of light depend upon two opposing facts:

1. That the skin arrests completely and absorbs certain light rays, especially the ultra-violet;

2. That the skin is penetrated by certain light rays, especially the yellow, red and inner infra-red.

Rationale of the Curative Effects of Light

Scientific research has not yet fully revealed the secret of the healing power of light. A review of the physiologic effects of light clearly indicates its powerful influence upon all vital processes. The energy of the sunlight is one of the things essential to animal and vegetable life, and when so applied as to secure its full effects, this form of radiant energy has the power to influence the major vital functions of the body in such ways as the natural healing processes are promoted, thus aiding the organism in its battle against disease, or rather in its struggle to restore and to maintain the integrity of its functions under abnormal conditions. All nutritive metabolic processes appear to be encouraged by applications of light.

The most active ultra-violet rays, 2,900 A. to 3,000 A., penetrate not more than one-tenth of a millimeter, or 1/250 of an inch, but the red and yellow and inner ultra-red rays penetrate much deeper, and to these rays must undoubtedly be contributed a considerable part of the beneficial effects observed from light applications, if not the chief benefit, as held by Sonne. It is certainly an error to credit to the ultra-violet rays the total therapeutic effects resulting from light applications.

Sonne holds as the result of careful research that the beneficial effects of light are chiefly due to the influence of luminous heat rays in raising the local temperature of the blood in the

68

blood vessels, which his remarkable experiments have shown may be accomplished to the extent of several degrees and without affecting the general temperature.

According to Saidman, the effects of ultra-violet light are photo-electric; that is, the light rays cause the molecules of the tissues to discharge negative electrons. This action is analogous to that of the beta rays. It is known that ultra-violet rays falling upon gold and other metallic bodies cause them to throw off negative electrons. Numerous facts tend to support this view.

The latent period which follows the application of light before the appearance of erythema is a phenomenon common to the X-ray and the ultra-violet rays, agents which are capable of ionizing the living cells.

Pigmentation is produced by radio active bodies such as mesothorium as well as by ultra-violet light.

The effects of the ultra-violet light upon the blood may be due to the secondary beta rays produced in the tissues by ultra-violet light. This theory explains also the sensitization by fluorescent substances since Christen has shown that beta rays are produced wherever fluorescence occurs.

Photo-Thermotherapy

In the theories advanced to explain the physiologic and curative effects of light, its heat effects seem to have received little attention. As a matter of fact, in the use of natural sunlight, or the arc light, heat rays are always dominant in quantity and a factor which must be reckoned with. It is of course true that the specific effects of heat are not always desired. When the effects of the ultra-violet rays alone are desired, care must be taken to suppress the effect of the heat rays. In the use of natural sunlight, when the treatment is given in the open air, it is only during hot weather, or especially warm days, that this factor requires consideration; but in the use of the arc light, the question of heat must always be given consideration. This fact the writer noted more than 30 years ago and solved the problem by combining with the arc light the use of an electric fan. By means of the fan, it was found possible to eliminate the heat factor so far as desirable to do so, by cooling the surface treated. It was also found possible by means of the fan, to greatly increase the intensity of the light applications without producing unpleasant heating effects.

It is evident, then, that in the practical application of phototherapy, a full appreciation of the thermic effects of light is essential. This is true not only of the sun bath but especially in the use of the arc light and of the electric cabinet bath.

In the employment of the incandescent light, either as a local or a general application, the thermic influence is practically the only effect obtained or expected, and so a knowledge of thermotherapy becomes of paramount importance.

The Physiologic Effects of the Thermic Rays (Luminous and Infra-Red)

The following summary of the general physiologic effects of heat, the writer takes the liberty to quote from his own chapter on Thermotherapy in "A System of Physiologic Therapeutics":*

"The *primary effects* of heat are those of an excitant or a physiologic stimulant. Within physiologic limits, the application of heat to living cells increases the activity of their protoplasm, an effect easily recognized in the quickened movements of the amebae, leukocytes, and other minute animal forms, when placed upon a warming stage under the microscope. Heat is thus one of the most powerful of all vital stimulants, exciting the function of all tissues upon which it may be brought to bear—glands, nerves, nerve-centers, and the like.

"These effects, however, are temporary, and are followed by *secondary effects* of an opposite character,—depression,—a sort of negative or atonic reaction after the withdrawal of the hot application. To these secondary depressant or atonic effects are attributable the weakening or exhausting effects of thermic measures when improperly managed or inappropriately applied.

*System of Physiologic Therapeutics, Vol. IX, P. Blakiston's Sons & Co., Philadelphia (1902).

"These mixed effects are due to the different functions of the various structures which are directly excited by the elevation of temperature following the immediate contact with a heated medium. Elevation of temperature of the sweat-glands and nerv structures heightens their activity. If the application of heat is continued for a sufficient length of time to raise the temperature of the blood, all the vital activities of the body are accelerated. At the same time, however, there is set in operation a series of inhibitory effects which result from the stimulation of the heat-nerves, the tendency of which is to lessen heat-production and lower blood pressure, and diminish the disposition to and the capacity for mental and muscular activity. Cold acts in precisely the opposite way. In lowering the temperature of the structures of the skin, it acts as a depressant, diminishing the activity of the sweat-glands and other structures. If continued long enough to lower the temperature of the blood, heat-production and other forms of vital activity are lessened. Cold acts, however, as an excitant to the cold-nerves of the temperature sense. (These nerves as well as others may be paralyzed by an intense or prolonged application of cold.) Stimulation of the cold-nerves reflexly produces strong excitation of almost every bodily function. The force of the heart contraction is augmented, the blood pressure is raised, heat-production increased, metabolic activity quickened, and the disposition to and the capacity for mental and muscular activity heightened. The effects of heat are, then, directly excitant, indirectly depressant; while the effects of cold are directly depressant and indirectly excitant. These mixed effects afford opportunity for an infinite number of variations in the form and intensity of hydric and thermic applications, and in therapeutic effects.

"The actual effects of a thermic application depend (a) upon its temperature, duration, and form; and also (b) upon the condition of the patient.

"A *prolonged application at a high temperature* is at first excitant, and then decidedly depressant. The excitation is the natural result of the elevation of the temperature of the blood. The depressing effects appear to result from the lowering of the nerve tone and the exhaustion of nervous energy by overstimulation.

"A *very brief application at a high temperature* is strongly excitant, and the depressing effects which follow may be so slight as to be quite imperceptible.

"A *less intense* and *moderately prolonged* thermic application is excitant to a moderate degree at first, depressant effects appearing later, after the conclusion of the application.

"A very complete statement of the physiologic effects of thermic applications upon the various bodily organs and functions has been given elsewhere in this volume, by Professor Winternitz (see pages 18 to 38) in a discussion of hydrotherapy. As the principles of thermotherapy rest upon the same foundation, it will be necessary to discuss here only such points as relate specifically to hot applications, and especially those which require somewhat fuller elucidation.

Effects of Heat Upon the Skin

"A very brief and very hot application produces a goose-flesh appearance from contraction of the smooth muscle-fibers of the skin.

"Heat contracts the yellow elastic tissue, but relaxes the white fibrous tissue that constitutes the chief element of ligaments and tendons.

"Heat may cause increase in perspiration to more than twenty times the ordinary amount.

"Tactile sensibility increases at 98° F. (36.7° C.); decreases at 113° F. (45° C.); and disappears at 130° F. (54.4° C.), when painful sensations are experienced.

"Momentary pallor occurs when the temperature is high (110° F.—say, 43° C.—and upward), and is quickly followed by reaction, with reddening of the skin from dilatation of the vessels. Lower temperatures produce immediate reddening of the skin with dilatation of the small blood vessels, especially the veins. Contraction of the cutaneous vessels, with pallor, occurs some little time after the withdrawal of heat, the result of atonic reaction and chilling of the surface from evaporation.

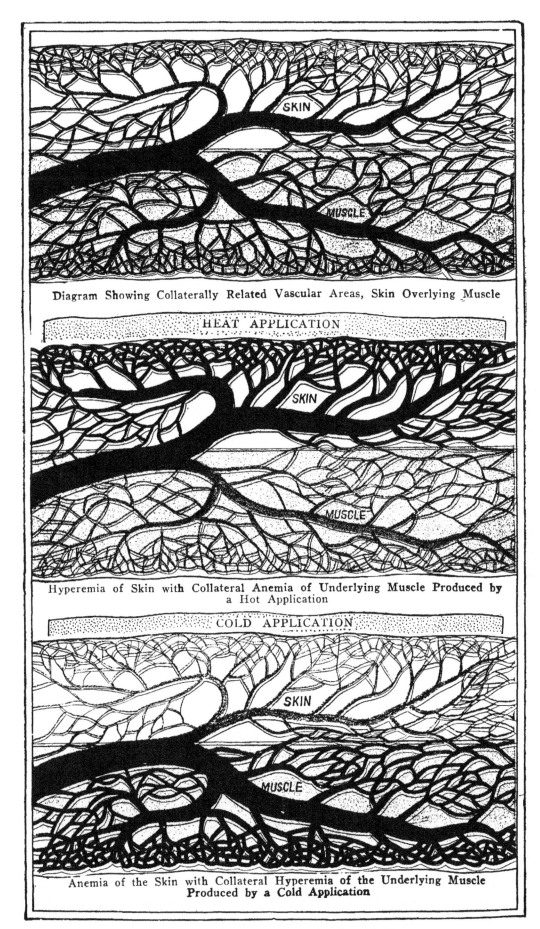

Diagram Showing Collaterally Related Vascular Areas, Skin Overlying Muscle

HEAT APPLICATION

Hyperemia of Skin with Collateral Anemia of Underlying Muscle Produced by a Hot Application

COLD APPLICATION

Anemia of the Skin with Collateral Hyperemia of the Underlying Muscle Produced by a Cold Application

EFFECTS OF HEAT UPON THE SKIN

"Following a hot application there is increased heat-elimination, which is the result of the quickened movement of blood through the skin, dilatation of the surface vessels, increased conductivity of the skin, and the more active evaporation occasioned by the great amount of moisture thrown upon the surface by the sweat-glands.

Effects of Heat Upon the Muscles

"The energy of the striated muscles is increased by short, hot applications.

"Prolonged warm or hot applications lessen the excitability and energy of voluntary muscles. It is thus that heat becomes of service in relieving muscular cramp. Cold produces the opposite effect.

"Very hot applications—104° to 130° F. (40° to 54.5° C.)—increase the excitability of smooth or involuntary muscles.

Effects of Heat Upon the Nervous System

"Very short hot applications excite the brain, nerves, and nerve-centers through the impressions made upon the skin.

"Prolonged general hot applications may give rise to pronounced exhaustion of the brain and spinal cord. Warm and hot applications lessen general nervous sensibility to a remarkable degree. This is especially true of very hot applications. The effect may be due in part to the absorption of moisture by the terminal nerve filaments in the skin; or it may be brought about by the stimulation of the temperature nerves. It is well-known that the skin is much more sensitive to thermic impressions than to any other form of stimulus that it is capable of recognizing.

"Applications of heat to the skin generally produce an agreeable sense of comfort and well-being. If the application is continued too long, languor, lassitude, and depression result.

"Very hot applications of short duration, like brief cold applications, have both a direct and a reflex excitant effect.

Effects of Heat Upon the Circulation

"Heart.—In general, heat applied over the heart tends to quicken the systole, while cold produces the opposite effect.

"General hot applications at first slow the pulse, then increase its frequency. Cold produces exactly the opposite effect.

"Blood Vessels.—Very hot applications at first cause the blood vessels to contract, then to relax.

"Under the influence of heat the *skin* quickly assumes a dusky red hue from slowing of the cutaneous circulation. The vascular activity accompanying the reaction which follows a cold application concerns the arteries especially, and gives the skin a bright red hue. The vascular dilatation due to heat is passive, while that due to cold is active.

"*Large arterial trunks* are dilated by hot applications prolonged sufficiently to heat the intervening tissues, or made at points at which large vessels lie near the surface, as in the groin, the axilla, the neck, the bend of the elbow, and the popliteal space.

"The principle of *derivation* or *revulsion,* which furnishes the foundation for one of the most important therapeutic uses of heat, depends upon the fact that, when the vessels of one portion of the peripheral area supplied by an arterial trunk are in a state of dilatation, the vessels of the remaining portion or portions are contracted. In other words, the local hyperemia induced by an application of heat gives rise to a compensatory or collateral anemia in correlated vascular areas. This explains the relief afforded by an application of heat about a rheumatic joint, or over an inflamed or congested nerve or muscle. The same fact likewise affords an explanation of the relief of visceral pain which results from a general hot application.

"Blood Pressure.—Cold raises blood pressure, while general hot applications lower blood pressure, though the blood vessels may be dilated in both cases.

"The dilatation which is part of the reaction following a cold application does not lower blood pressure, being accompanied by increased vigor of the heart's action resulting from reflex stimulation and increased activity of the small vessels—termed by some writers the 'skin heart,' but for which I prefer the name of the 'peripheral heart,' because the arterioles of the muscles and of various internal organs are influenced as well as those of the skin. A *very hot* application may raise blood pressure by reflex excitation of the heart, producing a quick, strong pulse; but in general, *hot* applications lower the blood pressure by dilating the cutaneous vessels and thereby lessening peripheral resistance. The skin is capable of holding from one-half to two-thirds of all the blood in the body. Hence, a general hot application, by dilating the surface vessels, and especially the veins of the skin, withdraws a large amount of blood from the internal circulation. The pressure in the ventricles of the heart is reduced, and the cardiac contractions are lessened in force.

"A *hot douche* produces an elevation of blood pressure, at the same time dilating the surface vessels to the fullest degree by its strong mechanical or percutient effect.

"The *tension of the tissues,* as well as that of the blood vessels, is diminished by the mechanical influence of heat upon the connective-tissue and muscular elements which form the framework of the tissues, and upon the unstriped muscle-fibers found in the skin and in most of the viscera.

The Effects of Heat Upon the Blood

"General hot applications diminish the number of red cells. Local applications of heat, either moist or dry, produce a very marked increase in the number of leukocytes, although reducing the number of red cells. Heat also lessens the alkalinity of the blood, thus diminishing vital resistance, as has been shown by Charrin. This fact emphasizes the importance of concluding every general hot application with a general cold application of some sort, the effect of cold serving to maintain the normal alkalinity of the blood, and thus to increase vital resistance. When profuse sweating is induced, the volume of the blood is diminished, unless the loss is made good by the ingestion of water.

Effects of Heat Upon Respiration

"Heat and dryness of the air hinder the gaseous exchanges in the lungs, and render respiration more frequent and superficial. Heat and moisture to the point of saturation interfere with elimination through the lungs.

"A *general hot bath* increases the rate and frequency of respiration. The depth of respiration is at first diminished; but if the bath is continued sufficiently long to raise the temperature of the blood, and increase carbon dioxid production, the respiratory movements are augmented.

"A frog breathes with its skin; a dog sweats with its lungs; man not only sweats with his skin, and breathes with his lungs, but, like the frog, to some extent, breathes with his skin, and, like the dog, sweats with his lungs. Hot baths promote not only the perspiratory activity of the skin, but also the elimination of moisture through the lungs, thus aiding the escape of those toxic substances which, as Charrin has pointed out, are probably eliminated through the bronchial mucous membrane.

The Effects of Heat Upon Body-temperature

"A *general hot bath* at a temperature above that of the body causes elevation of the temperature of the blood by interference with heat-elimination. For example, in a series of experiments in my laboratory, the temperature of a young man weighing 108 pounds was increased 3.2° F. (1.8° C.) in thirty minutes, representing an accumulation of 88.2 calories, by a bath at 100° F. (say 38° C.). A bath at the temperature of the body (98.4° F.— say, 37° C.) caused a rise of 0.6° F. (0.3° C.). Baths at a neutral temperature of 92° to 96° F. (33° to 35° C.) did not elevate the body-temperature. A Russian bath of twenty-five minutes' duration raised the temperature 2.1° F. (1.16° C.). An elevation of the same amount was observed as the result of an electric-light bath lasting twenty-three minutes. A rise of 1.7° F. (0.94° C.) resulted from a Turkish bath of one hour at 146° to 158° F. (63° to 70° C.). The increase of body-temperature induced by prolonged hot baths is not wholly due to diminished heat-elimination, since it has been shown that in dogs exposed to a temperature of 104° F. (40° C.) heat-production is augmented to three and one-half times the normal.

"A *short application of heat* is followed by a fall of temperature, the result of increased heat-elimination through dilatation of the surface vessels, and a diminution of heat-production through the reflex influence of the thermic nerves upon the thermogenic processes.

The Effects of Heat Upon the Abdominal Viscera

"As already observed, heat lowers the tone of voluntary muscles, while cold raises it. In other words, heat relaxes muscles, while cold contracts them. This effect is particularly marked when applications are made to the muscles of the abdominal wall, a fact which has long been taken advantage of in the treatment of strangulated hernia, and more recently in the practice of examining the pelvic and abdominal viscera while the patient lies in a hot bath.

"The *tension of the abdominal muscles* is a matter of no small importance in relation to respiration, and especially to the blood movement in all the viscera lying below the diaphragm. With relaxation of the abdominal muscles intra-abdominal tension is diminished, and the portal vessels become engorged with blood. All the viscera are congested. The stomach and intestines become distended with gas and their walls yield to the tension, resulting in dilatation, with stasis in the stomach and colon, and gastric indigestion and constipation, accompanied by fermentations and putrefactive processes that lead to autointoxication and various disturbances of nutrition.

"*Cold,* when applied to the abdominal wall, contracts not only the external voluntary muscles, but the internal, involuntary muscles of the stomach and intestines, urinary bladder, and gall bladder, together with the muscular structures found in the spleen and liver, and the muscular walls of the blood vessels. *Hot* applications to the abdominal walls produce the opposite effect. It is apparent that hot applications of this sort are therapeutically valuable for the relief of conditions of muscular spasm, either in the external voluntary muscles, or the internal involuntary muscular structures, as, for example, in intestinal or renal colic, and gall-stones.

"*Long-continued warm applications* to the abdominal surface appear to lead to concentration of blood in the portal circulation, doubtless by relaxing the visceral vessels.

"*Very hot applications* divert blood from the internal viscera by widely dilating the surface vessels. This effect is made possible by the anatomic connection that exists between the cutaneous vessels and those of the viscera, and which will be mentioned in detail a little later.

"By the alternate application of heat and cold, the *blood movement* through any internal viscus may readily and almost perfectly be controlled. Cold contracts the visceral vessels by reflex action through the thermic nerves, while heat produces the opposite effect. By the alternation of these effects a veritable pumping action may be instituted, whereby functional activity may be heightened, and morbid processes profoundly influenced.

"*Very hot water,* when brought in direct contact with the gastric mucous membrane, excites both motor and secretory activity, producing also a very decided stimulating effect upon the heart. *Cold applications* to the epigastrium, as well as cold applications to the general surface, increase the peristaltic movement of the stomach and stimulate the secretion of gastric juice. *Very hot applications,* either general or local, unless greatly prolonged, produce similar effects. It should be noted, however, that when the general hot application is prolonged until profuse perspiration has been induced, the secretion of gastric juice is greatly diminished. Puschkin has asserted from experimental observation that the amount of the gastric juice and its digestive activity are greatly increased by the application of heat to the epigastrium after eating. Results observed during more than a score of years, in the large use of this measure as a means of promoting digestion, enable me to say that Puschkin's claims are fully corroborated by clinical experience. Applications, to be beneficial in this way, must be very hot. Warm applications doubtless tend to diminish the secretory activity of the stomach and to lessen activity.

The Effects of Heat on the Liver and the Spleen

"According to the exact observations of Kowalski, *hot applications* over the region of the *liver,* followed by cold applications, increase the secretion of bile. This effect is doubtless produced by the increased movement of blood through the organ induced by an application of this sort, the rationale of which has previously been explained. The beneficial results obtained in hydriatic practice by the employment of fomentations over the liver, followed by the heating compress, fully corroborate Kowalski's conclusions. For more than a hundred years this measure has been employed, largely empirically, but nevertheless successfully, in the treatment of hepatic affections, especially catarrhal jaundice, so that it cannot be doubted that the liver may be influenced powerfully by this means.

"The effect of *thermic applications*—hot, cold, or alternately hot and cold—over the *spleen* is clearly shown in the rapid diminution in size which may thus be brought about in cases of splenic enlargement from malarial infection and allied conditions, when not involving definite structural changes in the organ.

The Effects of Heat Upon Renal Activity

"General hot baths promote renal activity, and increase the amount of urine when the temperature is sufficiently high to increase blood pressure—104° to 110° F. (40° to 43° C.). Renal secretion is diminished, however, when a general hot application is prolonged sufficiently to induce profuse perspiration. The powerful influence of general hot applications upon the kidneys is shown by the remarkably beneficial results obtained by the employment of the hot bath and other general hot applications in the treatment of acute nephritis.

The Effects of Heat Upon Metabolism

"General applications of heat, if sufficiently prolonged to elevate the temperature of the blood, increase carbon dioxid production. Nitrogen oxidation appears also to be particularly favored by the elevation of temperature induced by general hot applications.

"Experiments show that the elevation of temperature induced by general hot applications aids the body in the formation of alexins and antitoxins. Animals suffering from infectious diseases live longer when subjected to the influence of moderate heat. The recognition of this fact has led to the revival of the dictum of Hippocrates, that the elevation of temperature that occurs in connection with most acute infectious diseases is, within limits, remedial in purpose and effect. By parallel reasoning, we are led to the conclusion that a slight degree of pyrexia artificially induced by a general hot application may be beneficial in aiding resistance to infection, especially when followed by a short cold bath.

"Local applications of heat in many instances operate beneficially by increasing the blood supply of the affected parts as well as by greatly increasing the proportion of leukocytes."

Derivative Effects of Radiant Heat

The writer desires especially to call attention to a therapeutic principle which so far as known has not been definitely recognized in phototherapy, namely: the therapeutic value of the effect produced upon the skin by the thermic rays of the sun, of the electric arc, the incandescent filament, and other incandescent bodies.

One of the effects of heat upon the skin is to dilate the peripheral vessels. Just how this is accomplished it may be impossible to explain with certainty. The most recent and most plausible theory is that there are in the small vessels longitudinal as well as circular fibers which by contracting serve to increase the lumen of the vessels. This effect is produced by heat applied to the skin in any manner or from any source, as by means of a hot bath, a heated object brought into contact with the skin, hot air, and heated vapor, as well as by heat in the form of radiant energy; but radiant heat is unquestionably more effective than any other form of heat in producing this dilatation of the vessels because of its greater penetrating power. The rays of energy pass through the skin and penetrate to a considerable depth, being converted into heat as they meet with resistance. A more rapid and profound effect is thus produced by the heat of the sun, or from an arc light or incandescent filament, than by thermic applications of other sorts.

Heat Inhibits Pain

Another important effect produced by heat is pain inhibition. Acting through the temperature nerves, heat lessens nervous irritability and thus becomes one of our most precious means of combating pain. The same inhibitory influence may be employed as a means of lessening functional activity in an overacting organ. It is for this reason that we apply heat for the relief of spasm, as in colic and muscular cramp, and to produce muscular relaxation by lessening the excitability of the muscular tissue, thus lowering its "tone." The general depressing effects of heat, which are easily made manifest by a hot bath, are well-known. The fomentation owes its value as a means of relieving pain in many cases to this inhibitory effect, as in neuralgias, and especially in visceral neuralgias.

The effects of heat above mentioned are, of course, temporary. The vascular dilatation rarely persists more than an hour or two after an application of heat, no matter how prolonged, and not infrequently is followed by a contraction of the vessels and very pronounced anemia. This may be due either to the chilling of the surface from evaporation of the moisture which is always present in increased amount in consequence of the stimulation of the sweat glands, or to the natural reaction which follows over-stimulation of any sort, or both influences combined. The inhibitory effect produced by heat is also more or less transient. Nevertheless, both these effects are exceedingly valuable, and the effect of solar heat and heat from other luminous sources in dilating the vessels of the skin is of immense therapeutic importance in dealing with chronic maladies.

Pigmentation of the Skin by Heat

One of the very noticeable effects of the daily application of heat to the skin is a coloration and very pronounced mottling, or pigmentation, which always appears after heat has been applied daily for a few weeks. The longer the application the more pronounced the effect. This effect affords positive evidence of the very pronounced and permanent dilatation of the cutaneous blood vessels which results from thoroughgoing thermic applications.

The mottled appearance referred to differs from the tanning produced by the actinic or ultra-violet rays. The latter produce a uniform dark brownish tint, while heat rays produce a mottled coloration which often endures for weeks after the treatment has been discontinued.

A more intense and permanent effect upon the cutaneous blood vessels is produced by the ultra-violet rays of sunlight and the arc light when applied with sufficient intensity to produce so-called sunburn, or *solar erythema*. The intense reddening of the skin which appears usually within ten or twelve hours after a sufficiently prolonged exposure to intense actinic rays, is evidence of complete relaxation of the vessels of the skin and filling of these vessels with blood to an extraordinary degree. The skin is capable of holding, when these vessels are fully distended, one-half to two-thirds of all the blood in the body.

This fact sufficiently emphasizes the difference in the volume of blood contained in an anemic skin and one in which the vessels are fully distended. The therapeutic significance of this fact lies in the influence which congestion of the skin exercises upon the blood volume of internal parts. If the blood supply of the skin is within a short time increased from a small fraction of the total blood volume to one-third or one-half of the whole amount of blood contained in the body, it is evident that we possess in artificial congestion of the skin a method whereby we may quickly withdraw from the great vascular organs of the trunk from one-fourth to one-half of their total contents, thus affording almost instant relief to a congested liver, engorged spleen, hyperemic lungs, inflamed stomach or intestines, or congested spinal cord.

Vascular Relations of the Skin with Internal Parts

Careful study of the blood supply of internal organs in relation to the skin shows that the blood vessels of every important internal organ are very directly connected with the vessels of the skin, through arteries or veins, or both; so that it is possible to produce effects by means of local as well as general hyperemias of the skin, thus inducing collateral anemia of vascularly related parts. In his *Rational Hydrotherapy*, and in the chapter on Thermotherapy in *International System of Physiologic Therapeutics*, vol. ix, the author has summarized the anatomical facts respecting the vascular relations of the skin with internal parts. The liberty is taken to quote from the last-named work the following paragraphs:

"The vessels of the brain are freely connected with those of the scalp and of the nose through the parietal foramen, the foramen cecum, the mastoid foramen, the posterior condyloid foramen, the foramen of Vesalius, the foramen ovale, the foramen lacerum medium, the carotid canal, the anterior condyloid foramen, as well as through the diploë of the cranial bones.

"The circulation of the lungs is collaterally related with that of the skin covering the arms, the chest and the upper part of the back. The pericardium and the parietal pleura of the anterior portion of the chest are collaterally related with the skin covering the anterior portion of the chest wall through the internal mammary artery.

"The parietal pleura of the posterior portion of the chest and the visceral pleura are collaterally related with the intercostal vessels. A collateral relation also exists between the bronchial arteries, the nutrient arteries of the lungs, and the intercostals, especially those of the right side. The skin covering the arms is collaterally related with the pleura of the upper and anterior portion of the chest through the subclavian artery. There also exists a collateral relation between the nutrient vessels of the lungs and the vessels covering the anterior portion of the neck through the inferior thyroid arteries. The collateral relationship existing between the vessels of the skin and of the lungs is still further extended by the connection of the bronchial veins with the azygos veins of the right side, and with the superior intercostal or the azygos veins of the left side. It is in the highest degree interesting to note these extensive communications between the pulmonary circulation and that of the cutaneous surface, all of which are of high therapeutic interest.

"The kidneys are associated with the skin covering the loins through the renal branches of the lumbar arteries.

"The vessels of the prostate in man, the uterus and ovaries in women, and the bladder in both sexes, are associated with the cutaneous vessels overlying the sacrum, the buttocks, the perineum, the external genitals, the groins, the inner surfaces of the thighs, and the supra-pubic region, these parts being chiefly supplied by branches of the internal iliac artery. These parts are also associated with the skin of the leg through the common iliac artery.

"The rectum is similarly associated with the skin covering the anal region and the perineum and that of the lower extremities.

"There is a collateral relationship, both venous and arterial, between the stomach, liver, spleen, intestines, and even the pancreas, and the skin of the trunk which overlies those deeply seated organs.

"The portal circulation communicates with the systematic circulation, thus establishing a collateral relationship with the cutaneous vessels at half a dozen or more points, especially the following: the hemorrhoidal plexus, the esophageal veins, the left renal vein, the phrenic vein at the surface of the liver, the epigastric veins at the umbilicus, the circumflex iliac vein (Treves, Schiff).

"In a similar way it may be stated that the upper half of the body is collaterally related with the lower half; a fact of which

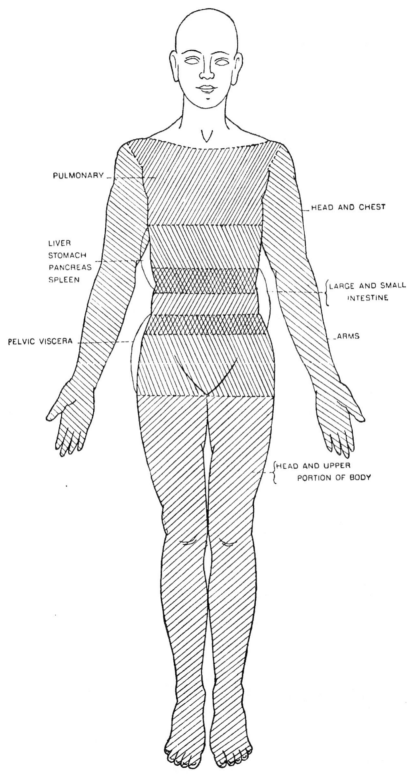

PULMONARY

HEAD AND CHEST

LIVER
STOMACH
PANCREAS
SPLEEN

LARGE AND SMALL
INTESTINE

PELVIC VISCERA

ARMS

HEAD AND UPPER
PORTION OF BODY

DIAGRAM SHOWING RELATION OF SUPERFICIAL TO DEEP CIRCULATION

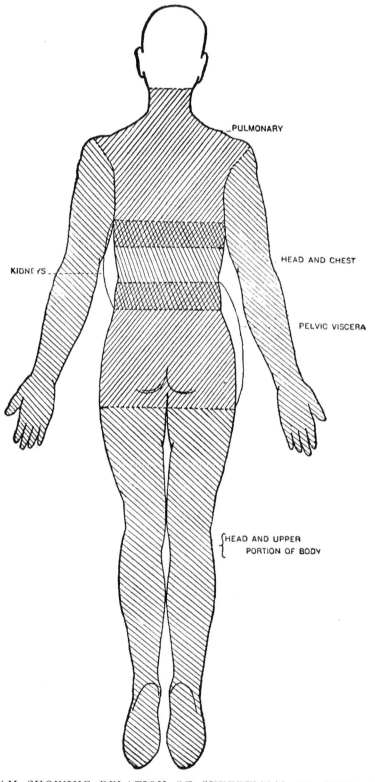

PULMONARY

HEAD AND CHEST

KIDNEYS

PELVIC VISCERA

{ HEAD AND UPPER
PORTION OF BODY

DIAGRAM SHOWING RELATION OF SUPERFICIAL TO DEEP CIRCU-
LATION—POSTERIOR

constant use is made when the lower extremities are warmed to divert blood from the head.

"The cutaneous vascular areas connected with the several viscera are roughly indicated in the accompanying diagrams. It should be remembered, however, that every portion of the cutaneous surface is vascularly related, at least remotely, to every internal part. It is also interesting to note that the vascular areas connected with the several internal viscera do not altogether correspond to the reflex cutaneous areas connected with the same parts, although in the main the reflex areas and the vascular areas are practically identical. For example, the skin covering the front of the chest is of greatest importance as a means of reflexly influencing the pulmonary circulation; whereas, the cutaneous vessels of the skin covering the back of the chest are more intimately related with the vessels of the lungs than are those of the anterior surface. A most important reflex relation exists between the skin covering the lower portion of the sternum and the kidneys, whereas the principal vascular relation exists between the kidneys and the skin covering the loins.

"The portion of the body below the umbilicus is collaterally related with the head, the arms and the upper half of the trunk; and the legs are likewise in collateral relation with all parts of the body above them, especially those which occupy the pelvic cavity."

Relief of Visceral Congestion

Phototherapy is a useful means of producing local and general hyperemia of the skin for relief of the visceral congestion which is rarely absent in chronic disease. The pallor of the skin which is nearly always present in chronic invalids signifies not only anemia of the skin, but necessarily implies also congestion of the viscera. When the vessels of the skin are in a state of chronic spasm, especially when the skin is in that "hide-bound" condition which indicates deficient development of the subcutaneous tissue, there is necessarily a surplus of blood in the internal parts. The general muscular weakness which accompanies chronic disease prevents exercise, so that the muscles as well as the skin are anemic. The importance of this fact will be recognized when it is considered that the muscles when active are capable of holding one-half of all the blood in the body. The idle muscle contains not more than one-fourth or one-sixth as much blood as the active muscle. A pale skin and inactive muscles necessarily imply congested viscera.

This chronic congestion of vital organs necessarily results in derangement of functions, and often in change of structure. Passive congestion or stagnation of the blood in a part necessarily involves diminished oxygenation and accumulation of CO_2 and other toxic substances in the tissues. The result is partial asphyxiation and autointoxication of the congested parts through the accumulation of tissue poisons. A congested liver cannot do its duty as a bile-making and toxin-destroying viscus.

The congested stomach first manufactures an excessive quantity of highly acid gastric juice, but with a deficiency of pepsin. Sooner or later the acid glands are worn out and hypopepsia and apepsia result. The stomach then becomes a culture chamber for microbes of various sorts. Under the influence of the toxins produced, glands degenerate, resistance is lowered, chronic gastric catarrh develops, cancer and other neoplasms appear; through absorption of the toxins formed, the resisting power of the blood is lowered; general autointoxication occurs and various cachexias develop; skin diseases of various sorts and general and local nervous disorders appear, especially the various forms of neurasthenia. Even melancholia and paresis may be traced to the influence of toxins generated in the alimentary canal.

Similar results may follow congestion of the intestines. The resulting catarrh of the duodenum may extend into the liver and gall bladder, giving rise to jaundice, gallstones, hepatic abscess, pancreatic disease, appendicitis, hemorrhoids, the various forms of colitis, mesenteric tuberculosis, tubercular peritonitis, cancer of the intestines and peritoneum, and other maladies which are the outgrowth of lowered general and local vital resistance and traceable to a blood supply which has deteriorated by long retention in over-dilated vessels.

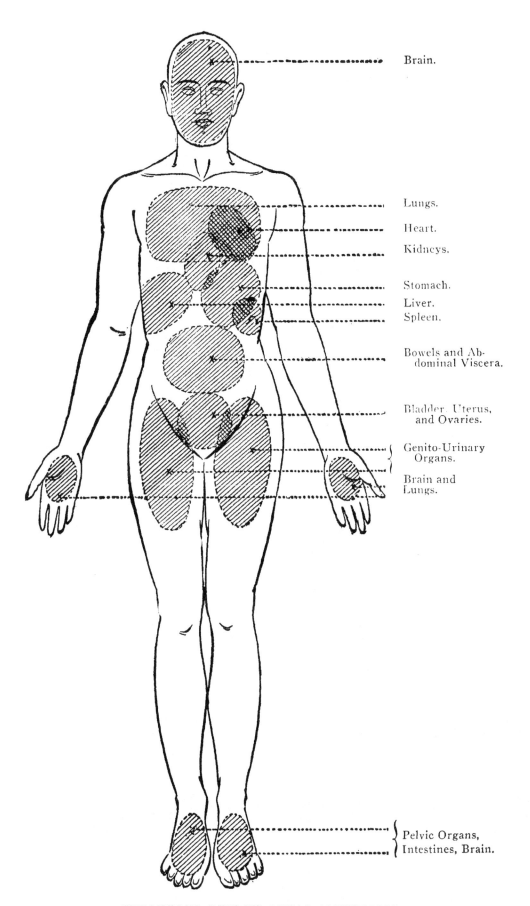

Brain.

Lungs.

Heart.

Kidneys.

Stomach.
Liver.
Spleen.

Bowels and Ab-
dominal Viscera.

Bladder, Uterus,
and Ovaries.

Genito-Urinary
Organs.

Brain and
Lungs.

Pelvic Organs,
Intestines, Brain.

CUTANEOUS REFLEX AREAS (ANTERIOR)

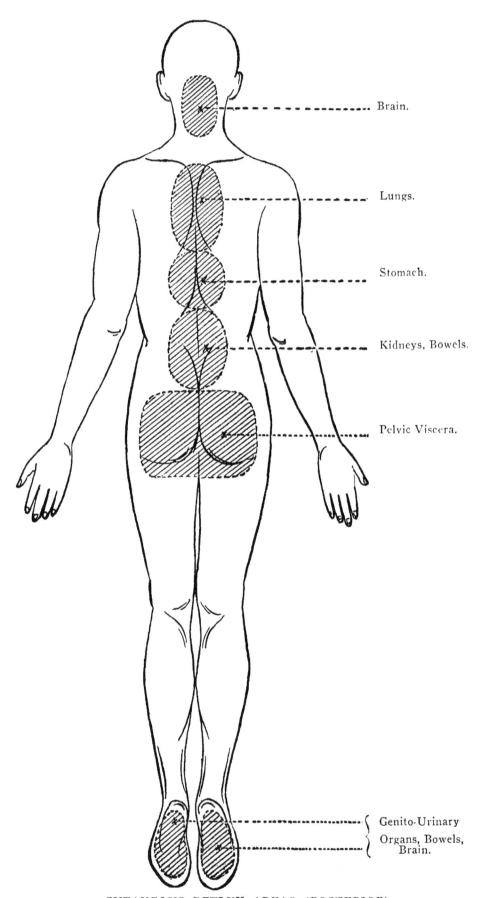

Brain.

Lungs.

Stomach.

Kidneys, Bowels.

Pelvic Viscera.

Genito-Urinary
Organs, Bowels,
Brain.

CUTANEOUS REFLEX AREAS (POSTERIOR)

Congestion of the sympathetic ganglia gives rise to abdominal pains of various sorts and a great variety of reflex pains and other symptoms, pain in the back, head, and limbs, paresthesias, neuralgias, and an almost infinite variety of mental and general nervous symptoms, vertigo, mental confusion, depression, pseudo-apoplexy, nervous irritability, nervous exhaustion, morbid fears and the *tout ensemble* of morbid phenomena presented by the vast proportion of neurasthenics and neurotics, both men and women.

Relations of Certain Cutaneous Areas with Reflexly Related Organs

Every portion of the cutaneous surface is in special reflex relation with some internal organ or vascular area. The most important of these reflex relationships are the following:

(1) The skin of the scalp, face, and back of the neck is in reflex relation with the brain. The circulation of the scalp is also immediately connected with the brain through the medium of the skull, the vessels of which anastomose with those of the scalp and those of the brain.

(2) The skin of the back is reflexly related to the centers of the spinal cord. This is also true of the entire skin surface of the trunk and limbs.

(3) The skin covering the neck is reflexly, through the spinal cord, related to the pharynx and the larynx.

(4) The upper dorsal region, the skin of the chest in front and behind, and the inner surface of the thighs, have special vasomotor reflex relation with the lungs.

(5) That portion of the chest wall overlying the heart (the precordia) is especially associated with the heart,—a fact often of priceless service.

(6) The skin covering the lower portion of the right chest is reflexly related to the liver.

(7) The skin surface of the lower left chest is associated with the spleen.

(8) The skin covering the lumbar region is reflexly associated with the uterus, ovaries, bladder, rectum, kidneys, and intestines.

(9) The skin covering the lower part of the sternum is especially associated with the kidneys.

(10) The dorsal spine is associated with the stomach, a fact which may often be made of great service in the suppression of nervous vomiting.

(11) The skin of the epigastrium has a special relation with the stomach.

(12) The whole surface of the abdomen, and especially the umbilical region, is reflexly related to the intestines.

(13) The lower abdomen is associated with the uterus, bladder, colon, and rectum.

(14) The feet, and to a considerable extent the whole lower extremities, are associated with the brain, lungs, bladder, uterus, ovaries, and bowels.

(15) The skin covering the shoulders and upper portion of the back and the arms and hands is an area which is closely associated with both the cerebral and the pulmonary circulations, and may be employed in producing most useful therapeutic effects both by the reflex influence of cold applications and by the derivative effects induced by heat.

The vessels of the important viscera may be caused either to dilate or to contract by cold applications to the skin, according as the application is short and intense (dilation) or long and moderate (contraction). Application of the arc light or the photophore to various skin surfaces, followed by or alternated with an application of ice or cold water or accompanied by ice rubbing at intervals, produces alternate dilatation and contraction.

The Technique of Light Applications

Light, whether from natural or artificial sources, like water, lends itself readily to great variation in modes of application. It differs from water, however, in the fact that its applications are of necessity practically confined to the surface. It is through its influence upon the skin glands, nerves and blood vessels that its varied effects are chiefly produced. The various applications of light naturally fall into four classes:

1. Sunlight.
2. The arc lamp.
3. The incandescent lamp.
4. The quartz lamp.

The Supreme Value of Sunlight

Sunlight is perhaps the most potent therapeutically of all forms of light energy. Unfortunately, however, in most temperate climates this source of light is quite unreliable. A cloud may cover the sun at just the moment when its energy is wanted for use. Changes in the character of the atmosphere also modify in a very decided manner the intensity and activity of the solar rays. Only in the Rocky Mountain region and the southwest portion of the United States can sunlight be depended upon for systematic use. There are, however, in most parts of the United States a considerable number of sunny days which afford a convenient opportunity for the utilization of solar energy for therapeutic purposes. The following is a description of the technique and indications in the use of sunlight for the treatment of disease :*

The Sun Bath

Since the clothing, or at least a considerable part of it, must be removed, it is usually necessary that a special place or apartment should be prepared for the administration of this bath. The

---

*This account of the sun bath is borrowed from the writer's chapter on the subject in the *System of Physiologic Therapeutics*, Volume IX.

sun bath is best administered in an outdoor gymnasium, provided with suitable couches, a sand bank, and other appliances. Several patients of the same sex may be treated at once in such an inclosure, the demands of modesty being satisfied by the scantiest of bathing attire. Male patients commonly wear very small trunks, jock-bands, or narrow loin cloths. A very convenient protective garment may be made of a small towel by attaching at each corner a tape twelve or sixteen inches long. The towel is passed between the thighs and each end is attached to the waist by tying the tapes together in front and behind. If white or light-colored garments are worn, a considerable amount of light will reach even the covered portions of the body.

When it is desired to expose the entire skin surface,—and this is always an advantage,—tight screens may be placed about the patient in such a way as to protect him from observation while permitting the sun's rays to fall directly upon his uncovered body. Small, roofless cabinets may be arranged upon a flat roof. A very efficient sun bath may be given in almost any sickroom which is so situated as to admit the sun's rays between 9 A. M. and 3 P. M., by taking out the window-sash and placing the patient nude on a bed or cot before the open window. In cold weather the patient may be placed before an unshaded window glazed with vita glass or helioglass.

Technic.—Either the whole surface or any desired portion of the body may be exposed to the action of the sun's rays. As a rule, it is best that the head should be protected. This may be accomplished by shading the head with a parasol, or by lightly covering it, first, with a moist towel, then with some dark-colored fabric. Exposure of the head sometimes causes nausea and other unpleasant symptoms through overexcitation of the brain and central nervous system, the natural result of the great penetrating power of the solar rays. This excitation is not necessarily due to overheating of the brain, but to the influence of the chemical or actinic ray, which is a powerful nerve stimulant.

When the whole surface of the body is to be exposed to the direct rays of the sun, it is sometimes well to protect the cerebral circulation still further by applying to the face, or to the neck and

BATTERY OF SUN-ARC THERAPEUTIC LAMPS IN USE AT THE BATTLE CREEK SANITARIUM

face, a cheesecloth napkin wrung out of water at 60° to 65° F. (15.5° to 18.3° C.) In the case of children and men the whole hairy scalp may be moistened as well as the face. When the exposure is continued for more than a few minutes, the wet napkin should be renewed one or more times. After a person has become accustomed to the bath, this precaution is unnecessary, and it is not often required except in case of feeble patients, and those who are very susceptible to the stimulating effects of the sun's rays.

In the treatment of various local affections which are especially amenable to phototherapy, it is seldom necessary to limit the action of the solar rays to the affected part, as great benefit may be nearly always derived from the general improvement in metabolism induced by the application of light to the entire cutaneous surface. When localized applications are considered necessary, however, the exposure may be confined to the affected parts. I have found it convenient, in these cases, to employ white sheets or blankets as a protective, as this secures at least a partial exposure of all parts of the surface.

Feeble patients will necessarily recline during the application. More vigorous patients may walk about in an outdoor gymnasium or solarium, and may even engage in light gymnastics of some sort, or gymnastic games, with advantage, especially when it is desired to increase oxidation to as high a degree as possible, as in obesity, diabetes, and the lithemic diathesis.

The duration of the bath will vary considerably, according to the patient, the season of the year, and the condition of the atmosphere. A feeble patient who has not been accustomed to the sun, should, at the first sittings, be exposed, at least to a very hot sun, for not more than three minutes; longer exposure is likely to produce headache, lassitude, insomnia, and depression. Such sensitive individuals are also very likely to be sunburned by a prolonged exposure. It is well to guard against this accident, for although not serious or permanent injury is likely to result, it is very disagreeable to the patient, and may discourage further efforts in a direction essential to recovery. The only treatment ordinarily required is the application of dry starch or a little zinc ointment; if there is considerable swelling, the cooling compress should be employed for a day or two. The sun baths need not be interrupted; it is only necessary to cover the affected parts during the application.

In persons with light hair and blue eyes—blondes—the skin is always thin and very sensitive. The skin of persons with dark complexion and dark hair,—brunettes,—and of those who belong to the dark-skinned races, is much less susceptible to the influence of the actinic rays, and hence less likely to suffer from overdoses of sunlight. In such persons the exposure may be prolonged to half an hour or even an hour without detriment. After considerable training it is possible, in fact, for the patient to expose the greater portion of the body to the influence of the sun's rays for several hours daily, not only without ill result, but with great benefit.

When the bath is applied daily, the skin rapidly acquires a brownish tint through the increase of pigment. The protection afforded by this pigmentation not only permits a longer exposure without injury, but also seems to make a longer application necessary to insure the desired results. I have often seen patients in the outdoor gymnasium whose naturally white skins had become as dark as that of a mulatto, or a half-caste Hindoo, or South Sea Islander. This darkening of the skin indicates approximately the metabolic and therapeutic activity of the solar rays. The intensity of the sun's rays is in north temperate latitudes very much greater during the three months from the middle of June to the middle of September, than in any other season of the year, increasing as the sun approaches the summer solstice, and diminishing as it recedes.

A clear or rarefied atmosphere also increases the intensity of the sun's rays. This fact should be borne in mind in the application of the sun bath in elevated regions. In the clear, rare atmosphere of a region elevated five thousand or more feet above the sea, the sun's rays are so intense that effects are obtained in half the time required at the sea level. To produce the best results, the sun bath should be taken daily, and the duration should rapidly be increased until the patient can bear exposure for from

A SUNSHINE PLAYGROUND

A SUNSHINE PLAYGROUND

thirty to sixty minutes at least once a day when the body is treated.

Partial Sun Baths

When it is desired to produce the more permanent effects which follow sunburn, it is better to expose circumscribed areas of the skin on successive days rather than the whole surface at once, as the patient is thus saved considerable discomfort. A sunburn involving the whole surface may produce profound disturbance in an over-nervous patient. By repeated applications the skin becomes very vascular, and intense pigmentation is produced, as is well shown in the accompanying illustration. One of the two subjects presented has just prepared to take his first light bath; the others have by daily exposure to the light become well tanned. In some instances the skin has been darkened to such an extent that the individual might easily be mistaken for a mulatto or an Indian if only the color of the skin were regarded.

The improved circulation of the skin which accompanies the pigmentation is always attended by relief from a multitude of disagreeable symptoms, and if these general light applications are supplemented by other indicated physiologic measures and by proper regulation of the diet and general habits of life, multitudes of cases incurable by other means may be, in the course of a few months, restored to excellent health.

Accessory Treatment

A *finishing treatment* of some sort is always required at the conclusion of a sun bath. This will differ according to the patient. In general, when the body has been heated sufficiently to cause perspiration, it is best to make a tonic hydriatic application.

The measures most serviceable in cooling and invigorating the skin, and in counteracting, by a general tonic impression, any depressing effect which may have been induced by superheating of the blood, are the cooling douche, the wet hand rub, the wet sheet rub, the shallow bath, the swimming-bath, and the alcohol rub, the application of which is later described in full.

Combined Sun Bath and Sand Bath

The sun bath combines well with the sand bath because the sand being made warm by previous exposure to the sun, the whole surface is equally heated, so that perspiration, with the maximum effects of the bath, is more rapidly induced. This is particularly true in the treatment of rheumatic individuals, who are especially benefited by sun bathing. Sufferers from chronic rheumatism, especially those whose joints are painful, should not receive a general cold application at the conclusion of the bath, but should be sponged with tepid water, placed in a sheet, lightly wrapped, and allowed to cool off gradually. Immediately after the sun bath the joints should be wrapped in cotton or wool and covered with mackintosh to avoid chilling by evaporation.

The Significance of Body-temperature.—The temperature of the patient should be taken before, during, and at the conclusion of the bath. The superheating which naturally results from an exposure sufficient to induce perspiration will be accompanied by an elevation of temperature amounting to one or two degrees Fahrenheit (0.5° to 1° C.).

Patients who do not perspire readily, naturally show a higher temperature than those in whom perspiration is easily induced. Diabetics; chronic dyspeptics with dry, sallow skins; chlorotics; and persons in whom the alloxuric diathesis is strongly developed, are especially subject to overheating, and hence require careful watching. Free drinking of water is a precaution that should be resorted to in these cases.

An ancient method of employing the sun bath, which is now obsolete, consisted in wrapping the patient in the skin of an animal and then exposing him to the intense heat of the sun's rays until vigorous perspiration was induced. A favorite place of making the application was the sandy beach of the seashore. After the bath, the patient was cooled off by plunging him into the cold sea.

Indications.—The sun bath is applicable in all forms of disease accompanied by defective metabolism, especially in conditions characterized by deficient oxidation, as obesity, diabetes, and the uric acid diathesis. The dry, sallow, leathery skin of chronic dyspepsia—an evidence of defective oxidation and profound auto-intoxication—rapidly becomes moist, lively, and velvety as the result of an hour's daily sunning. Neurasthenia, in all its forms, is materially influenced for good, the quality of the blood is improved, and all the tissue-building and energy-storing processes are stimulated. In anemia and chlorosis, the blood-making processes are encouraged, toxins are eliminated, and the spasm of the cutaneous vessels, which results in chronic visceral congestion, is rapidly relieved. In myxedema and exophthalmic goiter the sun bath is of great value when employed with proper precautions. In Bright's disease, in cirrhosis of the liver and in all other forms of visceral degeneration, patients often receive surprising benefit from this simple measure, when it is employed with proper adaptation to individual needs. In such affections great care must be taken in cooling the patient after the bath. In chronic rheumatism, rheumatic gout, and even in tuberculous joint disease, the sun bath often accomplishes wonders, always affording amelioration, and sometimes aiding the patient to recover in cases which seemed quite hopeless.

Winternitz years ago called attention to the great benefit that may be derived from exposing the skin to the sun in various cutaneous disorders, especially eczema. He covers the skin with a thin red cloth, and then exposes the parts thus protected to the influence of the full solar ray for some hours daily. Psoriasis also yields to this method. I have also met with success in several cases of chronic acne of the face and shoulders.

Contraindications and Special Precautions.—The sun bath is contraindicated in all febrile disorders, except in cases of chronic pulmonary disease with slight elevation of temperature. Decided febrile activity, however, should always be regarded as a counterindication to general sun bathing, or as necessarily limiting the exposure to a very few minutes, never long enough to increase the elevation of temperature. It should be remembered that in cases of this sort the thermotactic functions of the body are disturbed, and an elevation of the temperature is very easily induced.

In cases of insomnia, great care must be taken to avoid over-heating the head; the cold application following the bath should be carefully graduated, and at its conclusion a cold spray may be applied for ten or fifteen seconds to the legs and feet. In cases of rheumatism, gout, and rheumatoid arthritis, the cold application following the sun bath must not be too intense or too prolonged. It is often better to cool a patient, especially at the beginning of a course of treatments, by a tepid shower or fan douche or the broken jet. The temperature should be from 85° to 75° F. (say, 30° to 24° C.), and the duration twenty to sixty seconds. Care must be taken to avoid allowing the stream of cold water to fall directly upon the affected joints, as this will increase the pain. In cases of cardiac disease, in which there is marked evidence of failing compensation, prolonged exposure to the sun should be avoided, and the succeeding cold application should be very moderate in character, the temperature not being lower than 60° F. (say, 15° C.), and the duration from ten to twenty seconds. If the cold application is in the form of a douche, the precordial region should be avoided; the legs, the back, and the liver region receiving chief attention. In these cases, however, it is, as a rule, better to cool the patient by means of a cold towel rub or a wet sheet rub. When skin eruptions are present, very cold applications and friction must be avoided. The patient may be cooled by a prolonged rain douche at 85° to 78° F. (say, 30° to 25° C.), or a tepid bath at 90° to 85° F. (say, 32° to 30° C.), for two to six minutes. Reaction should in these cases be promoted by exercise after the bath rather than by friction.

The Arc Light—Its Special Advantages

There can be no question that sun bathing under favorable conditions is superior to any artificial means. Unfortunately, however, the most favorable conditions are by no means always obtainable. They are, in fact, generally inaccessible. One writer suggests the sun cure is a rich man's remedy. This is true to a certain degree, but it is likewise true that in most countries at certain seasons of the year the curative effects of sunlight may be made available to the rich and poor alike at almost no expense.

The increasing multitudes which throng our sea beaches everywhere during the summer season bear witness to the growing appreciation of the value of sunlight.

Unfortunately, in the countries which are occupied by the major part of the civilized portion of the human race there is a great deficiency of sunlight during the greater portion of the year and during the winter season sun bathing is quite out of the question. For this reason artificial light, which is really nothing more or less than resuscitated sunlight, becomes necessary as a substitute, and experience shows that the arc light may be successfully employed in place of sunlight and even possesses some advantages, among which the following are prominent:

1. The arc light, especially when metallic electrodes are used, is richer in ultra-violet rays; that is, it contains a larger proportion of short wave length rays than does the sunlight.

2. The arc light is of uniform strength and may be increased in intensity to any desirable degree, whereas sunlight is exceedingly variable, changing not only from day to day but from hour to hour, liable to interruption by clouds and lowered in intensity by dust and water vapor in the air.

3. The greater part of the year artificial light is so deficient in ultra-violet rays that pronounced effects are almost unattainable. In January, for example, the amount of ultra-violet rays in the sunlight is only about one-tenth that in July.

4. Natural sunlight is not easily available to the average individual. Opportunities for sun bathing are rare, especially for persons who live in cities. Provision should be made for sun bathing in connection with public schools in connection with outdoor gymnasia and swimming pools. But even these would be valuable for use only a part of the year, hence schools and public playgrounds should be supplied with facilities for artificial sunlight. This is already being done in some English schools and in a few schools in this country. By this means sunlight can be supplied every day of the year and at any time of day. Alpine and desert regions are about the only regions where efficient sunshine is always available. The apt suggestion is made by Amsted, of Leysin, that natural sunshine may be compared to a

crude drug of which the arc light is the refined extract. The arc light is, in fact, nothing more than resuscitated sunlight since it is produced by sun energy stored up ages ago.

5. Sonne has shown that the red and inner infra-red, that is, the thermic rays, both luminous and invisible, are the chief therapeutic elements of the light ray. The arc light, because produced at a lower temperature than that of the sun, contains a much larger proportion of red and infra-red rays than does sunlight. This fact demonstrates that the arc light may be at least as valuable as the sunlight, and in certain cases superior to it, as a therapeutic means.

6. The experiments of Steenbock showed that artificial light has a much stronger effect in the prevention and cure of rickets than has the sunlight.

7. Experiments at the Rockefeller Institute demonstrated the remarkable stimulating effect of light upon the endocrines, especially upon the sex glands. Steenbock has shown that artificial light greatly increases the production of eggs by fowls. Light has been shown to have a similar effect upon the production of milk by cows. Mellanby showed that ultra-violet light increases the activity of vitamin A, and Steenbock showed that artificial ultra-violet rays when applied to food deficient in vitamin D, give to the food the properties of vitamin D to a high degree.

To Avoid Depressing Effects of Heat

A point which seems to have been rather generally overlooked is also well worthy of notice, namely: that the highest degree of thermic stimulation through radiant heat may be produced upon the deeper structures of the body irrespective of the temperature of the skin surface or of the air surrounding the body. This is highly important for the reason that prolonged applications to the skin are depressing through the reflex effects which they evoke, whereas direct thermic applications are highly stimulating. For example, it is well-known that a hot application to the cutaneous surface through reflex action lessens heat production, whereas heating of blood increases heat production by stimulation of the tissues.

Heat is the most powerful of all vital stimulants. All bodily activities are increased under its influence. It is important, then, in all cases of slow metabolism and diminished oxidation, that we should be able to stimulate the processes of tissue change and the burning of tissue wastes without bringing into operation the reflex depressing effects which are produced by heating of the skin. The skin acts much like the glass roof of a hotbed. It permits the passage of the luminous heat rays which accumulate in the tissues because they become dark rays, and as such cannot be transmitted by the skin except by conduction.

The electric-light bath affords the only means by which this may be accomplished. Light rays pass through a cold skin as well as a warm one. It is important to know, however, that unless certain precautions are observed, this most desirable effect may be lost. For example, in the use of the incandescent electric-light bath cabinet, if the cabinet is closed, the air surrounding the patient will be quickly heated and so a certain amount of overheating may result. The heating of the air of the cabinet is never so great, however, as in the vapor or the Turkish bath. The perspiration induced in this bath is not the result of the heating of the air about the patient, but of the direct stimulation of the sweat glands by the thermic rays which penetrate below the surface.

Thus the peculiar and excellent quality of the electric-light bath here emphasized is always in operation to a greater or less extent; but to secure the full benefit of this special property of the electric light, measures must be taken to promote the cooling of the skin surface during the application. This may be accomplished in several ways. A simple means always available is the cooling of the surface by rubbing over it at frequent intervals a piece of ice, or quickly wiping it off with a sponge or cloth dipped in cold water. This method may be used in connection either with the arc light or the photophore. This is an extremely practical and useful measure, as it may be employed under any circumstances.

Still another and very effective means of cooling is the fan. This may be used by either of the methods illustrated in the accompanying cuts. The fan may be so placed that a strong current of air falls upon the surface to which the application is being made. The cooling effects of the air current may be enhanced by occasionally moistening the surface with a sponge or a wet cloth so as to increase the elimination of heat by evaporation. The effects obtained by this means have been found to be most excellent. The amount of radiant energy which is made to penetrate the skin is at least doubled, and yet the patient is not overheated.

A more convenient method of cooling the surface in connection with a general light application is the use of the electric fan in connection either with the upright or the horizontal cabinet, or the standing cabinet similar to that shown in the accompanying cut. In the standing cabinet the fan is placed at the top so that the current of air strikes first upon the patient's head, the exit being at the bottom. A thermophore is placed under the patient's feet.

In the employment of these combined procedures in which the skin surface of the patient is cooled during the bath, the blast does not in the slightest degree interfere with the application. In the use of an incandescent light cabinet supplied with 16-candle power lamps, at least a part of the lamps must be exchanged for 24 or 32-candle power lamps. When the arc light is employed, all that is necessary, of course, is to increase the amount of current.

Cooling the Skin During Light Applications Makes Intensive Applications Possible

By employing cooling measures so as to prevent overheating of the skin, the intensity of the light application may be greatly increased, and thus the effects upon the deeper lying tissues may be very considerably enhanced. The writer considers the combination of skin cooling with thermic stimulation of the deep-lying structures a most important advance in the light-therapy of chronic disorders. This measure is found particularly valuable in the treatment of a large class of cases suffering from chronic toxemia as the result of intestinal autointoxication. It is of equal value in the treatment of diabetes, obesity and various diatheses and cachexias.

This procedure combines the tonic or stimulating effects of cold and heat, while eliminating the depressing influence of both. Heat depresses through the inhibitory reflexes set up as the result of the overheating of the cutaneous nerves. Cold depresses by lowering the temperature of the blood. By the combination suggested, both of these depressing influences are eliminated, and the direct thermic stimulation of the deep structures produced by the deeply penetrating heat rays is combined with the powerful tonic reflex stimulation resulting from the cooling of the cutaneous nerves.

No possible combination of therapeutic forces could be happier than this. No physician who has witnessed the prompt and potent remedial influence of this combined procedure could fail to desire to make use of it.

By cooling the surface during a general light application, the range of application of the electric-light bath is very greatly increased, as it becomes possible to employ the bath in cases quite too feeble to endure it applied in the ordinary way.

Experiments made with the arc light combined with the air blast and without it give the following results:

In an application to one side of the abdomen for four minutes, the immediate effect was a very pronounced reddening of the surface. The patient experienced a very uncomfortable sensation of heat. The patient's position was then changed so as to allow the light to fall upon the opposite side of the abdomen. The air blast was turned on. The effect at the end of four minutes was very slight reddening of the surface and no discomfort from heat. The next day very pronounced solar erythema appeared on both sides alike. The skin was very sensitive. The effects were slightly more pronounced upon the side to which the air blast had been applied in connection with the light, than upon the other side, showing that the air light bath should be used when it is necessary to increase the intensity of the effects of the actinic ray. It is very evident that the air blast cannot interfere with the effect of the penetrating heat rays upon the deeper tissues, since the cooling effects of the air blast must be confined entirely to the cutaneous surface.

Water Drinking

In general, electric light applications should be preceded by water drinking. This is true even of the arc light applied to a comparatively limited area, for the reason that light applications always promote to a marked degree activity of the skin and hence diminish the volume of the blood through the loss of water. This is, of course, especially true in those applications in which vigorous perspiration is induced, as in the cabinet bath. A glass of water, either hot or cold, may be taken just before entering the bath, and if profuse perspiration has taken place, additional water should be given after the bath.

The Arc Light

The rays of the arc light may be applied either in diffuse or concentrated form to any portion of the body's surface. Its most important use is probably as a general application in the arc-light bath.

Requisites

The first requisite is a good arc light, conveniently arranged for therapeutic use. After examining all the therapeutic arc lamps offered on the market in this country and Europe, and finding all more or less objectionable because of inconvenience in use or unreasonably high price, the author had constructed under his supervision a lamp which, after several years of service in the Battle Creek Sanitarium, in hundreds of other sanitariums and hospitals, and in the offices of private physicians, has proved to be eminently satisfactory. The latest models of this lamp which was first to use the parabolic reflector (Solar Therapeutic Arc Lamp) is shown in the accompanying cuts.

Technic

The application must be made, of course, to the uncovered skin of the patient. The ordinary clothing of the patient may be loosened and arranged in such a way as to expose the part to which the application is to be made, or the patient may be undressed and covered with sheet and blankets. When the application is made to a large surface, it is always better that the patient should be undressed, especially when the treatment is to be prolonged, as more or less perspiration not infrequently attends the application, and this requires a general cooling measure of some sort to prevent the patient from taking cold afterward.

Care should be taken to maintain the temperature of the room at about 70° F., so that the tendency to perspire shall not be unduly encouraged. The patient may be seated in front of the lamp, or may lie upon a bed or couch.

The Solar Therapeutic Lamp is mounted upon a light but solid and easily portable stand, and is also provided with means of adjustment so that it may be readily adapted to the individual case, both as regards position and strength of current. It is, of course, more economical to place the patient as near the lamp as is convenient, as this will utilize the rays more economically and so prevent a waste of current.

After the lamp has been properly adjusted so that the rays fall upon the area to which the application is to be made, the current is thrown on by closing the switch, the rheostat being adjusted so as to regulate the current at minimum intensity. The current is then rapidly increased to the degree desired. Care is taken to note the moment of the beginning of the application so that the seance may be timed to meet the needs of the individual case.

It is important to warn patients who are unacquainted with the application that solar erythema is a possible consequence. This is especially true in relation to very light-haired persons whose skins contain little pigment and hence are very susceptible to the influence of the actinic rays, particularly when the application is to be prolonged more than three or four minutes and when the light has a considerable degree of intensity.

The duration and intensity of the application may vary from a very short seance of one or two minutes, barely sufficient to produce a slight reddening of the surface, to an exposure of half an hour. These long seances will, however, be applied only in cases in which the patient's skin has become accustomed to exposure to the light, so that a sufficient amount of pigmentation has been developed to protect the tissues from injury, and in cases in which it is desired to produce a decided erythema for derivative effects, as when the purpose is to relieve some deep-seated pain or internal congestion.

Here are a few suggestions, careful attention to which insures against failure in the use of the arc light:

1. Make use of an efficient apparatus. The flaming arc is indispensable for highly successful work.

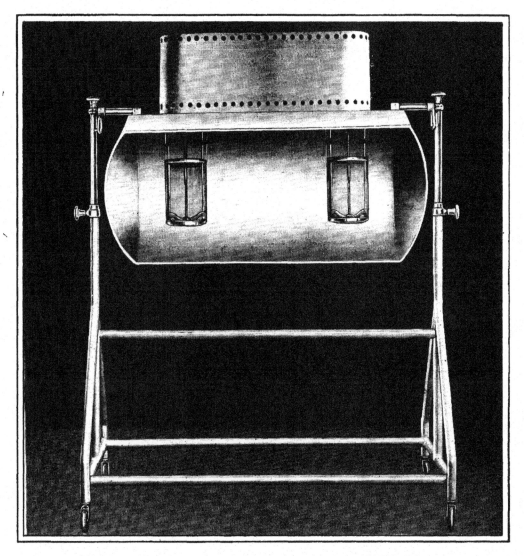

TWIN ARC LAMPS WITH REFLECTOR HOUSING

2. Test carefully the susceptibility of each case. Here are two methods:

(a) Prepare, of opaque material, a cuff or sleeve to slip over the forearm, with five holes, each about 3/4 of an inch in diameter (see cut). Expose the cuff covered arm to the light at the usual distance (usually about 30 inches). At the end of one minute, cover one of the holes. At the end of two minutes, cover another and so continue, exposing the last hole five minutes. After 24 hours examine the skin and note the effects of the different exposures. By this means the susceptibility of the patient may be properly judged, and the duration and intensity of the exposure may be intelligently regulated to meet individual needs.

(b) Another method of testing the sensibility of the skin is this: Draw the rubber end of a lead pencil across the skin of the chest or abdomen, employing considerable pressure. If a red welt rises almost immediately, the patient is subject to dermographism and is probably hyper-sensitive to light. It is well to employ both tests.

3. Avoid overdosage, but endeavor to secure a mild erythema effect at the first application (that is, in average cases). In feeble cases, expose only a small part of the body at the first seance, covering not more than one square foot if an intense application is to be made.

4. To intensify the effect and to shorten the time of exposure, warm the skin before the treatment by rubbing or by the use of the fomentation or the photophore.

5. Prepare the skin surface by a cleansing bath. Do not apply cold cream or any other fatty substance before exposing the parts to the light. Mineral oil may be used.

When it is necessary to restrict the light to a small area, the surface outside of the part to be treated should be protected from the influence of the light by means of dark or black cloth or paper. When the patient is facing the arc light, the eyes should always be protected by means of colored glasses. The eyes are very susceptible to the influence of the chemical rays.

The arc light is applicable to a great number of morbid conditions, especially when combined with proper hydriatic measures.

The Arc-Cabinet Bath

A very effective general light bath may be given by means of a single arc light and a portable cabinet similar to the vapor bath cabinet in popular use. The reflector of the arc lamp is placed at an opening made for this purpose in the cabinet. The patient, by turning his body, may receive the rays upon all sides, and by tilting the lamp the lower part of the body may easily be reached. By using two arc lamps the desired effects may be secured more quickly than with one lamp.

An Improvised Arc-Light Cabinet Bath

By the aid of two arc lights a very satisfactory arc-light bath may be improvised. The patient is seated upon a low stool, and an arc light is placed opposite the center of the trunk in front and another behind, opposite the center of the back. Two sheets are adjusted in such a manner as to cover all with the exception of the patient's head. (See cut.) By means of this improvised arc-light bath, as efficient applications may be made as by the aid of the most expensive cabinet, and the effects are much better than those obtained from cabinets arranged with a single arc light.

LOCAL APPLICATIONS OF THE ARC LIGHT

Technic of Local Applications

When it is desired to produce a powerful revulsive effect, ice should be rubbed over the surface at the completion of the application. A most intense revulsive effect may be induced by rapidly going over the surface with a piece of ice every minute or two during the application of the light.

It is always important to take great care that the surface treated is thoroughly dried after the application of cool water, alcohol or ice at the conclusion of the treatment.

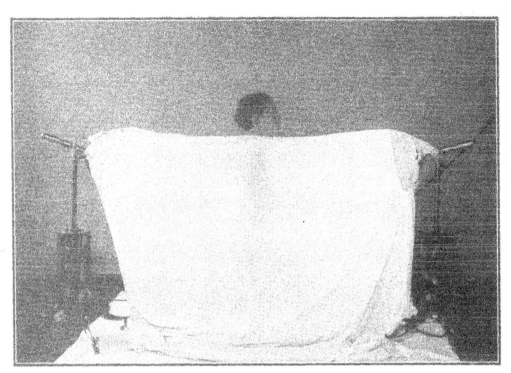

ARC-LIGHT BATH WITH TWO ARC LAMPS

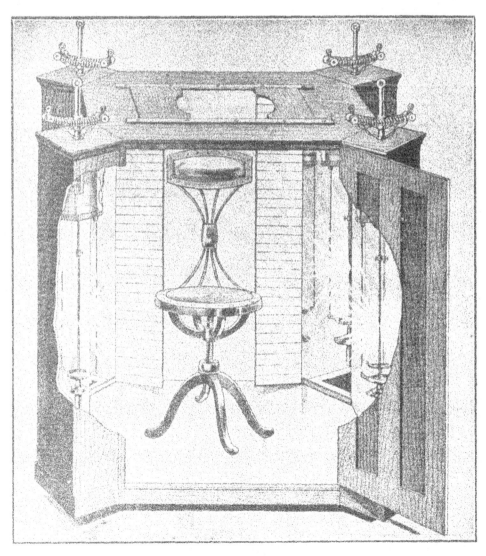

THE FIRST ARC-LIGHT CABINET BATH (1897)

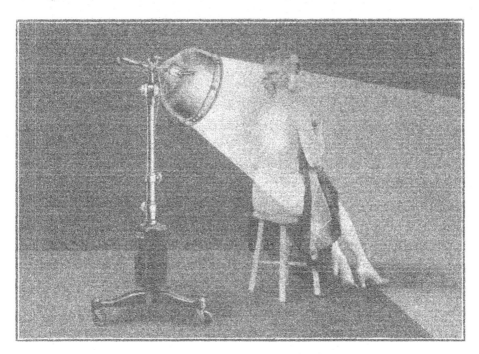

ARC LIGHT TO THE SPINE

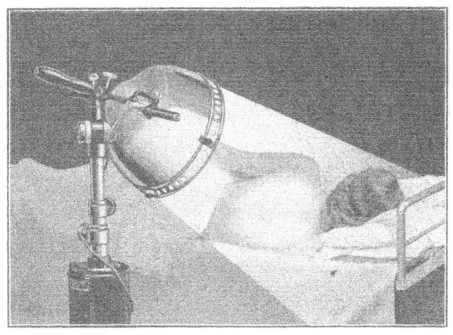

ARC LIGHT TO THE SPINE IN RECLINING POSITION

Arc Light to the Spine

The skin of the back is supplied with nerves which have their origin near the different spinal centers. This portion of the body is consequently one of the most important to which applications can be made, and through applications to this circumscribed area effects may be induced in every organ of the body, often the most distant parts.

With the clothing removed from the upper half of the body so as to expose the entire back, the patient is seated upon a stool or the side of a chair with the arms folded in front, so as to flatten the scapulæ and expose the skin of the back as fully as possible. The front portion of the trunk is protected by a sheet, as shown in the accompanying cut.

For a general application to the back, a Solar Lamp is now adjusted in such a way as to allow the parallel rays from the parabolic reflector to fall upon the upper portion of the back and the lower portion of the neck.

The intensity of the light may be adjusted either by regulation of the current or by the distance at which the lamp is placed from the patient. The regulation of the current by a rheostat is of course the most economical method.

In general the application should be sufficiently intense to produce a very decided sensation of heat. After a few moments, reddening of the skin will be observed, with perhaps the beginning of perspiration. This is an indication that the full effect of the application has been secured. The lamp should then be lowered so as to allow the rays to fall upon the lower half of the back until like effects have been produced.

When it is desired to confine the effects to the central portion of the back, as in certain forms of spinal pain, or to a single small area as in cases of tuberculosis of the vertebræ (Pott's disease), and in applications to circumscribed areas for the cure of cutaneous eruptions, the lamp should be adjusted by focusing in such a way as to concentrate the rays upon an area of the required diameter.

Local as well as general applications of the arc light, when of sufficient intensity to produce general perspiration, must be followed by a general tonic application.

The surface treated should be sponged off at the close of the application with tepid water, or rubbed with the hands dipped in cold water.

In cases of patients too feeble to sit erect, the application may be very conveniently made to the patient in bed or lying upon a sofa or treatment table. It is only necessary that the clothing should be removed and a sheet or other covering adjusted in such a manner as to protect the entire surface with the exception of the back.

Indications

Applications of the arc light to the spine are indicated in all cases of spinal pain whether due to disease of the vertebræ, neuritis or other diseases of the spinal nerves, or to disease of the liver, stomach, or other viscera—so-called referred pains. Applications of the arc light to the spine or back are particularly useful in cases of spinal hyperesthesia, referred tenderness due to gastric disease, gall-bladder disease and other reflex causes. The thermic rays of the arc light are among the most powerful means of pain inhibition yet discovered.

Solar erythema of the spine produced by the arc light is the most effective of all known means of producing derivative effects in relation to the spinal cord, and hence may be relied upon as a most effective means of relieving spinal congestion from different causes. The thoroughgoing application of the arc light to the back produces essentially the same effects as those produced by the fomentation, the thermophore and the electrophore, but very much more lasting.

Applications of the Arc Light to the Chest

The application may be made to the front of the chest or to one side, as shown in the accompanying cut.

The particular precautions necessary are to protect the eyes and the heart and to avoid making the application so long as to produce over-heating. In cases of very feeble patients when the heart is affected, a cooling coil or ice bag, covered with flannel, should be kept over the heart during the entire application. It is sometimes also wise to keep over the patient's throat a towel wrung out of ice water; in case this is done, the towel should be frequently renewed.

Indications

The indications for light applications to the chest are as follows:

Applications to the chest are valuable as a means of relieving pain in the chest, in intercostal neuralgia and pleurodynia. In pneumonia, pleurisy and acute bronchitis these applications are invaluable.

In the acute stage of bronchitis the application should be made for short periods only, not more than two or three minutes, and should be followed by the cold compress or the ice pack for twenty minutes, when the light application may be renewed. In pulmonary congestion from any cause these short, intense light applications to the chest are invaluable for producing derivative effects.

In cases of chronic bronchitis the application should be made in such a way as to produce a decided solar erythema. For this purpose, of course, an arc light is required. Applications of the photophore are also valuable, especially when made to the back. They may be renewed several times a day to advantage.

The application of the photophore to the back, accompanied by a cold compress to the chest, is an excellent means of relieving passive pulmonary congestion.

Very short applications over the heart are useful in cases of collapse under anesthesia, opium poisoning, and in cases of heart failure due to other causes.

Epigastric Application of the Arc Light

The arc light affords a most efficient means of relieving gastric and hepatic pain and congestion, whether acute or chronic. The accompanying cut shows with sufficient clearness the mode of application. The duration of the application may be made five to fifteen minutes, as there is very little danger of overheating. The patient enjoys the bath greatly and frequently experiences relief within a minute or two after the beginning of the application. The application should be repeated daily or even twice a day in cases of chronic gastric pain, and may be followed with advantage by the heating compress.

In cases of chronic gastric catarrh, chronic inflammation of the gall bladder, chronic duodenitis and cholangitis, it is well to produce solar erythema of this region, thus producing a permanent hyperemia of the skin, a most excellent derivative measure. This is an excellent means of relieving the gastric pain and heaviness which many chronic dyspeptics experience an hour or two after eating.

Application of the Arc Light to the Abdominal Region

This procedure is of special service in cases of abdominal adhesions resulting from peritonitis, also for the relief of pain and intestinal spasm due to chronic colitis. Also indicated in chronic appendicitis, in hyperesthesia of the lumbar ganglia of the sympathetis, in gastralgia, visceral neuralgia, gastric pain due to hyperhydrochloria and other non-inflammatory, painful affections of the abdominal region.

Applications of the Arc Light to the Loins

The application should be as hot as can be borne, and in severe cases should be continued long enough to produce a marked erythema.

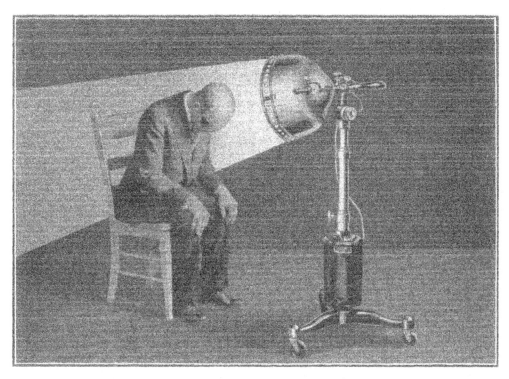

ARC LIGHT TO THE SCALP

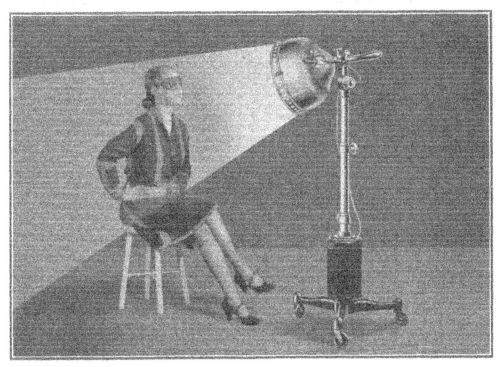

ARC LIGHT TO THE FACE

Indications

This application of the arc light is one of the best means yet discovered for relieving the pains of lumbago. It is, of course, not a radical cure for backache due to visceroptosis, visceral congestion, hemorrhoids, pelvic disease, colitis, chronic constipation and other abdominal disorders of which backache is a reflex symptom, but it is a most satisfactory measure for obtaining symptomatic relief. It may also be employed with excellent results for relief of pelvic pain, dysmenorrhea, amenorrhea, chronic metritis, salpingitis, ovarian neuralgia and various other pelvic disorders; in chronic prostatitis, neuralgia of the bladder, and inflammation of the bladder in both sexes; also in locomotor ataxia, spinal cirrhosis, chronic myelitis and various other organic disorders of the spine for palliative effects.

Application of the Arc Light to the Hepatic Region

There is probably no way in which the liver can be more profoundly influenced therapeutically than by a proper application of the arc light. The application should be made with the patient seated partly facing the lamp, but turned slightly to the left, as shown in the cut, so as to permit the light to fall upon the entire area of the skin which is reflexly connected with the liver, including the left lobe. The temperature should be as high as can possibly be borne, and in very chronic, obstinate cases, it is well to continue the application long enough to produce a decided erythema.

Indications

This measure is capable of rendering great service in many cases of chronic inflammation of the gall bladder and the biliary passages. It relieves pain and tenderness by lessening congestion and nerve sensibility. By dilating the surface vessels it diverts blood from the liver, opening up systemic channels for relief of the portal veins. This is particularly important in cases of cirrhosis accompanied by abdominal dropsy.

Application of the Arc Light to the Face

Care must be taken to protect the eyes with colored glasses kept closely adjusted so as to exclude the actinic rays, which might otherwise give rise to a very distressing conjunctivitis.

Indications

This is an extremely valuable remedy in the various forms of acne and other skin disorders. It is also an excellent means of relieving facial neuralgia and neuritis.

Application of the Arc Light to the Shoulders

This is a potent remedy for the relief of neuritis, which is so common in this region of the body; also in neurasthenia, rheumatism and other painful affections of the shoulder joints. It has a special value arising from the fact that it may be applied in cases in which fomentations and other moist applications can not be readily made without soiling or disturbing bandages or other dressings which may have been applied. A most excellent measure for use in cases of pain following dislocation or other traumatisms of the shoulder, and amputation of the breast for cancer.

Application of the Arc Light to the Hip and Thigh

The patient should lie upon a bed or couch with the clothing adjusted in such a way as to expose the buttocks and the outer and posterior portion of the thigh. The application should extend as high as the sacro-iliac synchondrosis. A napkin should be applied to the waist to protect the anus and the genitals.

Indications

This is a most admirable measure for use in relieving the pain of sciatica, whether acute or chronic. It is also useful in cases of rheumatism in the hip joint and the pain following fracture or dislocation of this joint.

Application of the Arc Light to the Scalp

In applying the arc light to the scalp, care must be taken to avoid overheating of the head. This may be easily accomplished by the use of the air-blast elsewhere described. The principal use of this application is to stimulate growth of the hair. It is, however, also an excellent remedy for dandruff. In many cases a copious growth of hair has been induced on scalps which had been bald for years. Of course, it is not possible to secure a luxuriant growth of hair upon a smooth and shiny scalp in which the roots of the hair have undergone complete atrophy and destruction, but in cases in which the scalp is covered with a growth of fine soft hair, excellent results may be sometimes obtained. The application should be sufficiently intense to produce a decided hyperemia.

The use of the arc light is also indicated in cases of neuralgia of the scalp, and to relieve headache due to cerebral anemia common in arteriosclerosis, some forms of Bright's disease, and in neurasthenics with low blood pressure. The arc light affords an excellent means of drying the hair after a shampoo, and promoting the growth of the hair. In studying the methods of Finsen, at Copenhagen, some years ago, the writer observed that the nurses employed in treating the patients presented a luxuriant growth of hair upon those portions of the hands and arms which were more or less exposed to the light of the powerful arc lamps.

Application of the Arc Light to the Knees and Other Joints

The accompanying cut shows the mode of applying the arc light to one or both knees, the feet and ankles, the elbows and hands.

Indications

Applications of this sort are extremely valuable in rheumatism, whether the result of repeated attacks of acute infectious rheumatism or from intense chronic intestinal autointoxication or so-called rheumatic gout. It is also an invaluable remedy, probably the best of all local applications that can be made, in cases of joint tuberculosis. It produces more intense and more prolonged hyperemia than Bier's method. A much higher temperature may be employed than by the hot-air method. The highly energetic ultra-red rays penetrate the tissues to a depth of more than an inch, whereas the effect of a hot-air application is confined to the surface of the skin. This is the special advantage of employing the active and energetic thermic rays associated with light instead of heat in the ordinary form in which it is applied by hot air or hot water.

The pain and tenderness of joints following sprains yield to the arc-light as to no other external application. The penetrating short-wave, thermic rays reach the painful, deep-lying structures which cannot be so well reached in any other way. The applications should be made daily and in many cases two daily applications are better than one.

Therapeutic Use of Photo Erythema

The effect of the actinic rays in producing a pronounced acute dermatitis, identical with that known as solar erythema when caused by the sun, has long been fully recognized as the result of the action of the ultra-violet rays upon the skin. The erythema, although called a sunburn or a light burn, is really not a burn at all, because it does not appear at the time of exposure, but several hours afterward. The more intense the application, and the longer the duration of the seance, the sooner the appearance of the erythema.

A decided reddening of the skin generally occurs when the arc light is used, but this is due to the dilation of the cutaneous vessels which results from the influence of the thermic rays in heating the skin. This redness usually disappears very quickly.

Photo erythema is of longer duration. When quite severe, and when covering a large surface, considerable inconvenience may be experienced for a few hours or even a few days; but there is never sloughing, ulceration or definite injury of the skin, as so often occurs with the X-ray, so the patient may be assured of the harmlessness of this symptom when it accidentally occurs.

The writer believes he was the first to make use of this effect of the actinic ray as a derivative and resolvent measure. For many years the production of erythema has been a distinct therapeutic aim in our treatment of selected cases, and especially in the treatment of cases of visceral disease, or of deep-seated pain, as in sciatica, and in joint affections accompanied with considerable exudation, in bad cases of acne and obstinate psoriasis. The results in these cases are most excellent, often brilliant, and highly gratifying to both patient and physician.

The writer has become fully persuaded that when employed for general therapeutic purposes, especially in cases of visceral disease, the full effects of the arc light are not obtained without the production of erythema.

As a means of producing pronounced and enduring hyperemia of the skin, this measure can not be excelled; indeed, it appears to have no rival except the rays of the midsummer sun.

Indications

The photo erythema may be induced for derivative effects with excellent results in a variety of visceral affections, especially in the chronic passive congestions of gall bladder disease, gastric catarrh, chronic enteritis, colitis, chronic appendicitis, and cirrhosis of the liver. In the last-named disease in particular, it is of singular service. In cirrhosis the portal obstruction leads to stasis in the splanchnic area, with impairment of all the intestinal functions. Dropsy occurs and marked increase of intestinal autointoxication. By producing a marked erythema of the whole abdominal surface, from the lower part of the sternum to the pubes, the systemic outlets of the portal circulation are widely opened, and thus the stasis is relieved to a very considerable degree.

Backache, lumbago, sideache, and many obscure and illy defined pains yield to the potent influence of the powerful inhibition of the thermic rays, combined with the filling of the cutaneous vessels by the lasting hyperemia induced by the actinic rays.

The Incandescent Light Bath

When the incandescent light bath was first constructed and introduced into therapeutics by the author in 1891, no adequate conception could be formed of the large place which this curative agent was destined to fill in the modern treatment of disease. Since that time the electric-light bath in various forms has found its way into almost all of the leading hospitals of the world. Hundreds of establishments, especially devoted to the employment of light as a therapeutic agent, have been opened, more particularly in Germany, and hundreds of physicians have become acquainted with the remarkable healing properties of this agent. Phototherapy or light-therapy has come to occupy a large field in therapeutics, and the number of papers, treatises and reports dealing with the subject has multiplied to an astonishing extent. The list of the maladies which yield to the influence of light is daily increasing, although including already quite a large proportion of the chronic ailments encountered in clinical practice.

Freund, of Germany, has been among the most active in developing the therapeutics of light. He employs the simple incandescent light apparatus with or without color filters in the treatment of superficial skin affections for neuralgia, myalgia, etc. The appearance of marked hyperemia and slight perspiration indicates that the treatment should be for the time suspended. Painful effusions of the joints and muscles and rheumatic pains are quickly relieved. This treatment quickens the reabsorption of serous joint exudations and dropsical accumulations. Rheumatic patients who can hardly stand before the treatment are able to walk without pain after it. Complete cure is effected when the treatment is prolonged and combined with other suitable therapeutic measures.

Exposure of superficial inflammations and suppurations to powerful incandescent lamps brings strikingly good results (Freund). This treatment is especially beneficial in cases of acne vulgaris, ulcerating X-ray dermatitis, ulcerating lupus, and scrofulous neck abscesses. The duration of the exposure was thirty minutes with the disease part as close as possible to the source of light.

Dworetzky, Kessler, Turner, Minin and others testify to the value of local treatment with the electric incandescent light in such painful affections as lumbago, rheumatism, cephalalgia, odontalgia, pleurisy, and pains in the chest following influenza; also in the absorption of exudates in cases of rheumatism, pleurisy, peritonitis, and gonorrheal arthritis. They even report good results in the absorption of effusions of blood, both retinal and subcutaneous and also subperitoneal. Ulcerations, eczema, lupus, and other skin affections, and venereal and syphilitic effusions heal more rapidly under the influence of local incandescent light.

Rockwell reported excellent results in the relief of pain dependent on congestive and inflammatory conditions even though deep-seated, and has found the light treatment to be far more efficacious in neuritis than any other therapeutic measure.

In addition to its power to relieve high blood pressure and pain, its thermic properties have a stimulant effect on metabolism, and its efficacy in increasing the hemoglobin-carrying power of the red cells renders the incandescent light valuable in a variety of conditions.

Schamberg thinks that light would doubtless have been more used as an auxiliary therapeutic measure had not the suddenly established reputation of the X-ray thrown the milder-acting light rays into the shadow. The X-ray produces important and profound changes in the cells and tissues, and when judiciously applied becomes a wonderful therapeutic weapon. But it is also capable of doing great harm, even irremediable, when improperly used. On the other hand, light energy, although much slower and milder in its effect, is perfectly safe.

Effects of the Incandescent Electric-Light Bath

During the time which has elapsed since its first employment (1891), this bath has been used under the author's general supervision in more than fifty thousand cases, aggregating several hundred thousand applications. At first its chief value was attributed to its eliminative effects, but deeper study of the subject has convinced the author that its chief value rests in its influence upon the circulation. Under the influence of the general electric-light bath, the skin is filled with blood. The stimulation of the sweat glands is incidental. The perspiration has some value through its influence upon general metabolism, but the amount of toxic matters carried out through the skin is small.

The complete filling of the skin with blood removes the disabling congestion of the liver, stomach, spleen and other internal parts. This relief is rendered more or less permanent by the fixation of the blood in the skin effected by the cold application which always follows the electric-light bath as well as other general heating measures. The active vascular dilatation following this cold application is of much longer duration than that resulting from the application of heat alone; thus a more or less durable effect is produced.

By a daily repetition of this procedure, normal conditions are gradually restored. The circulation of the skin becomes more and more active, and the amount of blood in the over-distended internal organs is diminished. The enlarged liver and enlarged spleen contract, the congested sympathetic nerve centers return to the normal state, and the vital resistance of the tissues is increased. Catarrhs of the stomach and intestines and biliary passages disappear, the digestive secretions acquire their normal characteristics, the liver, adrenals, and lymphatic glands and other poison-destroying organs resume their functions. The various symptoms of autointoxication disappear; the skin reacquires its natural elasticity and color, and the patient gradually returns to a normal state.

For producing the effects described, long applications are seldom necessary. Three to six minutes are ordinarily sufficient. The duration of the bath need be only enough to produce moistening of the skin from perspiration. In certain classes of cases, longer baths are needed. This is especially true of obesity, rheumatism, gout, and in diabetics who are strong and not emaciated. In these cases it is necessary to continue the bath sufficiently long to produce an elevation of temperature, so as to stimulate oxidation of the protein wastes. For this purpose the duration of the bath should be fifteen to thirty minutes, or until the temperature taken in the mouth reaches 100° to 100.5° F. It is better, when possible, to take the temperature per rectum.

The Incandescent Light as a Source of Infra-Red Rays

As a source of heat rays, the incandescent light is not excelled either for efficiency or convenience as a measure for therapeutic use. It has rapidly won its way to popular favor and has rendered obsolete the Turkish, Russian, vapor and other forms of heating baths which had been in use for centuries.

Therapeutic Applications of the Incandescent Light

During the thirty-six years which have elapsed since the writer constructed the first electric-light bath, he has found the field of application for this convenient thermic measure continually widening. This device has, indeed, proved to be of far greater value in the treatment of a large variety of maladies than any other means of applying heat, not excepting water, and admits of more general employment than the ordinary Turkish, Russian, vapor, or hot-air baths. One reason of this is the convenience and rapidity with which the degree of heat may be graduated by turning on or off one or more groups of lamps, the amount of heat being thus rendered absolutely and instantly controllable, since the source of heat relied upon is the incandescent filaments of the lamps rather than a heated atmosphere. The instant the lamp is turned off, the heat which had previously been emitted is withdrawn from operation. If additional heat is required, the desired number of lamps may be turned on, and become instantly operative. Still more perfect regulation may be effected by means of a simple rheostat.

Another reason for the more universal utility of the incandescent-light bath is the fact that when properly applied, its effects are highly tonic in character. A short application of the bath at full intensity for a time just sufficient to induce strong heating of the skin without provoking profuse perspiration, is a most effective means of cutaneous stimulation. The tonic effects of such an application may be still further intensified by instantly following the bath with a cold spray or other cold application, thus producing a revulsive effect of the most agreeable and effective character. The intense heating of the skin prepares the way for the cold application, without at the same time so overheating and relaxing the blood-vessels as to render recovery of the tone of the cutaneous tissues so tardy as to involve the risk of exhausting the patient too greatly or exposing him to the liability of taking cold. In the experiments referred to, the amount of perspiration produced in the electric-light bath was found to be double that produced in the Turkish bath. The body temperature is also raised much more rapidly in the electric-light bath than in any other form of hot bath, because the rays of radiant energy pass through the skin and reach the interior of the body at once, whereas in the ordinary hot bath the heat penetrates the tissues very slowly, and only reaches a small distance beneath the surface.

The electric-light bath is especially valuable in renal disease and in diabetes, in which prolonged sweating measures can not usually be employed without more or less risk. The penetrating nature of the heat of the electric-light bath stimulates oxidation of the residual tissues, and thus hastens the disappearance of redundant fat in *obesity*. In *dropsy,* associated with either cardiac or renal disease, in the *toxemia of chronic dyspepsia,* and in all conditions for which general and local applications of heat are applicable, the electric-light bath stands pre-eminent.

In *rheumatic* and *anemic* patients, and in all cases where the heat-making capacity is small, the electric-light bath serves an exceedingly useful purpose in preparing the skin for cold applications by storing up in it a supply of heat. And it serves a useful purpose in this way, not only in preparing the patient for tonic applications of water, but as a means of producing most excellent revulsive effects. For pure revulsive effects, only the circulatory reaction is desired, it being, in fact, necessary to suppress thermic reaction together. Hence, the duration of cold applications which follow hot applications should be such as exactly to neutralize the heat which has been absorbed by the skin in the previous hot application. The electric-light bath is superior to all others in the treatment of *chronic rheumatism* and all maladies dependent upon chronic toxemia, owing to its ability to elevate body temperature while at the same time producing vigorous cutaneous activity. The elevated temperature stimulates the oxidation of protein wastes, and augments vital combustions, while the increased skin activity carries off the waste products prepared for elimination.

Recent physiological experiments have shown that the elevated temperature in febrile conditions is one of the methods by which Nature combats the causes of disease, or neutralizes some of the morbid conditions resulting from disease. The physiological effects of the electric-light bath may exercise in many cases a strongly curative influence by the elevation of the body temperature, thereby enabling it to produce antitoxins, or to render more effective the curative efforts instituted by the *vis medicatrix naturæ*.

As a prophylactic, this bath also possesses a high value, especially for persons who live a sedentary life, as teachers, doctors, lawyers, preachers, judges, and professional men generally, and to a still greater degree for the majority of women, as it is the best substitute for muscular activity.

The hygienic value of the sweating bath is certainly scarcely yet appreciated by the majority of civilized men and women. This cannot be said of the Finns, however; for in Finland every house has connected with it a bath-house with conveniences for producing vigorous perspiration. Indeed, the author, while on a visit to Copenhagen, was told by an intelligent Finnish gentleman that it is the custom in his country for a young man anticipating matrimony to build as a foundation for his future home, first of all, a sweat-house. A vast multitude of city dwellers in civilized countries are suffering tortures from disease in various forms, and dying prematurely, because of the neglect of that important provision in the injunction of the Almighty to Adam, "By the sweat of thy brow shalt thou eat thy bread." Indeed, the neglect to sweat is one of many prolific causes of disease in the conditions of civilized life. A modern writer has very saga-ciously suggested that the chief difference between the savage and the civilized man is in the way he sweats. The savage sweats his brow in earning his bread, and taxes his brain but little; the civilized man earns his bread by the sweat of his brain, but sel-dom sweats his brow.

Sweating by the electric-light bath, while not a complete sub-stitute for the sweating produced by exercise, certainly comes nearer to being so than any other sweating process; and when fol-lowed by some vigorous cold application, as the cold shower, pos-sesses a hygienic value which cannot be overestimated.

Cautions and Contraindications

The electric light acts far more quickly than any other heat-ing procedure for the reason that its rays instantly penetrate deep into the tissues an inch or more, and thus the body temperature is quickly raised. It is well to take the patient's temperature just before the bath and immediately after, and even during the bath if it is much prolonged. In a prolonged bath the body tempera-ture may rise to 103° F. or more in a few minutes (15 to 20 min-utes). The general light bath should not be given to a patient who is in a febrile condition.

Intense heat is depressing, especially to the heart; hence it is necessary to protect the heart during the application by means of an ice bag or a cool compress.

The electric-light bath is too exciting for certain forms of skin diseases, especially when the eruption is moist and when intense itching or burning is present.

Technic of the Incandescent Light Bath

In the use of the incandescent light bath, either cabinet or photophore, the following points should be borne in mind:

1. The application is thermic in character, the amount of ultra-violet rays present being quite insignificant.

2. The purpose of the application is to heat not only the skin, but the sub-dermic tissues.

3. The intensity of the application is limited by the tolerance of heat by the skin. When the temperature of the cutaneous nerves is raised above 115°, pain is experienced and the limit of tolerance is reached at 120° F. By cooling the skin by means of a current of air, the intensity of the application may be very greatly increased. Sonne has shown that the rate of radiation of heat from the skin in cool air is increased to five times the normal. A current of air produced by an electric fan may be used in general applications with the light cabinet bath or, in local applications, with the photophore.

4. A glass of water should be taken just before the bath and after.

5. Care should be taken to see that the feet are warm.

6. Care should be taken to avoid overheating.

7. It is not necessary to cool the patient's head in the cabinet bath except in giving long sweating baths.

8. In general, prolonged sweating should be avoided except in certain cases of rheumatism and obesity. In such cases, the bath should be sufficiently prolonged to produce a rise of temperature of one or two degrees.

9. Applications of radiant heat should always be followed by a cooling procedure adapted to the case. Cabinet baths require a cool or tepid shower, a neutral bath, or cool towel rub or wet sheet rub.

Local Incandescent Light Applications

Local applications of light produce equally pronounced beneficial effects. Applications of the incandescent light may be made by means of the photophore, which consists of a metal cover enclosing one or more electric lamps. Lamps of any power desired may be employed. Care must be taken to protect the edge of the photophore if made of metal, so that the skin will not be burned. The author has had constructed photophores of various forms for application to different parts of the body. Some of these various forms are shown in the accompanying cuts.

These local applications are of special value as a means of applying radiant heat to the spine, the abdomen, and the joints. This is a much more effective means than any of the various forms of hot air apparatus which have recently been so extensively sold. A higher temperature can be borne because of the absence of moisture, and more exact results can be obtained, as it is not necessary to cover the skin and there is no possibility of setting the patient's clothing on fire; and, if reasonable care is exercised, there is no danger of burning the patient. It is not necessary to confine the air in the apparatus, as the heat is not in the air, but is produced in the tissues, radiant energy being gradually converted into heat as it meets resistance in the opacity of the tissues of the skin and underlying parts. The part to which the heat is applied may be made to tolerate an intense application for a long time by frequently passing the hand over the heated surface or by using an air current. The pressure of the hand facilitates the change of blood in the parts, thus cooling the overheated nerves while the penetrating rays of energy still continue their work.

The most remarkable of the therapeutic effects of light may be readily accounted for by principles which are well known to hydrotherapeutists, and without appealing to any theory of subtle, indefinable or hypothetical influence. It is not necessary to invoke the aid of any mysterious influence to find a rationale for the effects of light when employed therapeutically.

The Photophore

While the arc light is the most efficient and useful of all methods of applying light to the general surface of the body, the photophore is equally pre-eminent as a means of making local applications of heat. A radical defect in the hot-water bag and other means by which heat is conveyed to the body by contact, is the fact that from the moment the heated body is brought in contact with the skin its temperature steadily diminishes through the loss of heat. At the same time the tolerance of the skin for heat gradually increases as the contact is prolonged. This requires

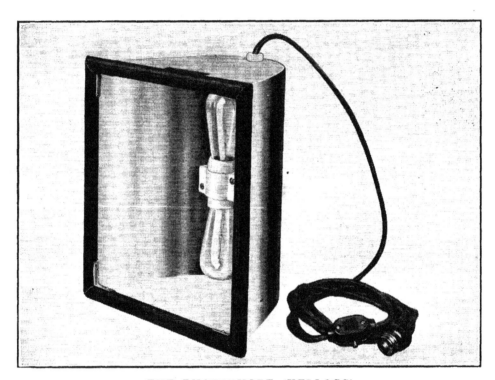

THE PHOTOPHORE (KELLOGG)

frequent renewal of the heat to produce a decidedly pronounced effect. The photophore entirely overcomes this difficulty. The volume and temperature of the thermic rays emitted from the incandescent film remain practically the same during the entire period of the application. The supply of heat being ample, the maximum effect desirable under the conditions is always attainable.

The photophore is made in varying forms and adapted to various uses. The capacity is also regulated by varying the size or number of the incandescent lamps employed. The accompanying cuts show some of the many different forms which have been designed for use in the Battle Creek Sanitarium, where this therapeutic appliance was first made and employed under the writer's direction, and where it has been in very extensive use during the last thirty-six years.

Indications

The photophore is one of the most effective means of relieving pain. The value of heat as a means of inhibiting pain cannot be overestimated. There are almost no forms of pain which are not greatly mitigated by the proper application of heat, and in the majority of cases complete relief can be obtained by a suitable application of heat by means of the photophore. For a fuller discussion of the subject of heat as a means of relieving pain, the reader is referred to the author's articles on this subject in Cohen's *System of Physiologic Therapeutics** and *Rational Hydrotherapy*, pages 265-269.

The accompanying cuts illustrate the application of the photophore to various parts of the body.

TECHNIC OF APPLICATION

The heat of the photophore is so intense that the skin may be easily burned if there is any loss of sensibility. Special care must therefore be taken to avoid too close contact or too high a temperature in cases in which the cutaneous sensibility is impaired.

---

*Volume ix, pp. 242-278. (Blakiston.)

When the application involves a large surface or is long continued, general superheating of the body and even perspiration may be induced, and hence proper precautions must be taken so that the patient may not take cold on going into the open air after the treatment. This is especially important in cold weather. In hot weather it is also important to avoid this general overheating by having the patient's clothing removed during the treatment.

In many cases it is well to place a cold cloth or an ice bag over the heart to avoid a depressing effect. The surface treated should always be cooled after the application by the sponge or hand-bath with tepid water. In cases in which the object of the application is to reduce a chronic exudate or to relieve tenderness or persistent pain, the application should be followed by the heating compress.

Powerful revulsive effects may be obtained by rubbing ice upon the skin at the conclusion of the treatment or at intervals of one or two minutes during the application.

The Incandescent Light Bath in Bed

By means of three two-light photophores an excellent incandescent electric-light bath may be administered in bed. The photophores and the patient should be arranged in the following manner: The patient being placed in bed, lying upon one side, a two or three-light photophore is applied on either side of him and another photophore at his feet. The patient and the photophore are then covered by a sheet and one or two woolen blankets, the covering being tucked in snugly about the neck and shoulders. The edges of the sheet and blanket may, if necessary, be attached to the mattress with safety pins to keep them from coming in contact with the body of the patient. After the bath has progressed for a few minutes the patient may think it desirable to turn upon the opposite side, to enable the light rays to act upon every portion of the surface.

An incandescent arc-light bath administered in this way is just as effective as when given with a larger and more expensive apparatus, though perhaps somewhat less convenient in applica-

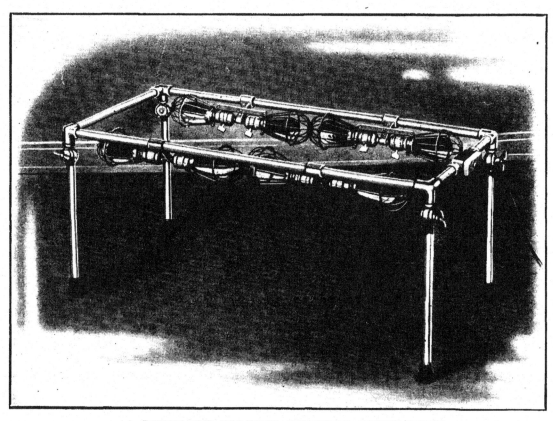

A PORTABLE FOLDING ELECTRIC LIGHT BATH

tion. However, there are many cases in which the patient is extremely feeble or otherwise unable to move from the bed to the bath or to sit upright in bed. In such cases the improvised bath in bed above described will be found an extremely satisfactory substitute for the usual form. This bath has also the advantage of being available in any room of a private home or hospital lighted by electricity. It is also economical in the use of current.

The Radiantor

A more convenient means of giving a general incandescent light bath to a feeble patient in bed is the radiantor, which has been especially devised for this purpose. (See accompanying cut). By the use of this light appliance, a light application may be conveniently made to the entire body or to the upper or lower half, as may be desired.

The Radiantor is especially serviceable in the treatment of bedridden cases of paralysis and chronic rheumatism and gout.

The Radiantor has proven of great service in the post-operative treatment of surgical cases, as a means of relieving pain after abdominal operations. Crile and others, as well as the writer, have called attention to the value of radiant heat as a means of preventing adhesions after abdominal sections. In the writer's experience, heat applied in this manner has rendered great service in the treatment of abdominal pains believed to be due to adhesions; and there is reason for believing that by a persevering use of this measure such adhesions may in some cases, at least, be made to disapppear.

The Combined Arc Light and Incandescent Bath

The combined effects of the arc light and incandescent light may be secured by two methods: first, by means of a cabinet in which are arranged both arc light and incandescent light; and second, by means of a window in the incandescent light cabinet through which the rays from an arc light may be introduced upon some particular area of the surface as may be desired. A small door for this purpose may be arranged in the door of the cabinet, or the door of the cabinet may be opened and the light projected into the cabinet. Applications of this sort are usually made to some portion of the abdomen or back. By this combined method the most powerful effects known to phototherapy may be obtained.

The Hand Photophore

This convenient instrument, here shown, is especially useful in cases in which it is desired to employ the highest temperature possible. In application the photophore is held in the hand with the elbow properly supported, and the rays are made to fall in succession upon the different parts of the area to be treated, by simple rotation of the arm, causing the photophore to describe the small arc of a circle of which the hand and forearm are the axis. By this means a much higher temperature can be borne than when the application is continuous, and thus more powerful inhibitory effects may be induced. This measure is especially useful in the treatment of sciatica and lumbago and other forms of chronic neuralgia, especially in the shoulders, back and other parts.

Intensive Applications for Relief of Pain

The use of heat as a means of relieving pain is one of the oldest therapeutic measures. Even suffering animals seem to be guided by instinct to resort to this simple physical agent when suffering pain. A dog suffering from earache puts his warm paw against his ear. A baby with earache places its hand to its ear. A person suffering with abdominal pain involuntarily bends his body forward and draws his thighs upward. Primitive people of all countries from the Arctics to the South Sea Islands treat rheumatism by hot vapor or steam baths administered in various ingenious ways. The Finlander shuts himself in a small room and creates steam by pouring water on hot stones. The Maoris of New Zealand heat stones in a pit and cover them with palm leaves on which the patient lies down, and a mat is covered over all.

Just how heat relieves pain is perhaps not fully understood. It probably acts in several ways, sometimes by diverting blood from congested parts through the production of a collateral

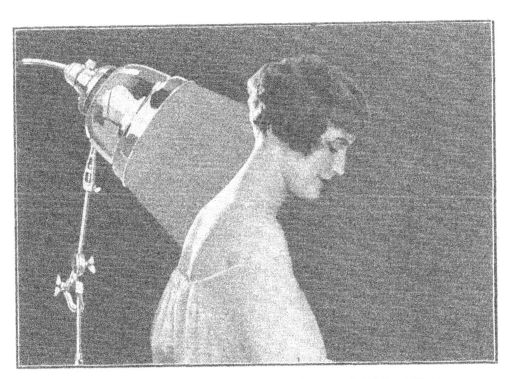

APPLICATION OF PHOTOPHORE TO UPPER SPINE

hyperemia, and sometimes, perhaps, by accelerating blood movement and so relieving a vascular stasis. But almost magical effects in relieving pain are often produced by hot applications under conditions in which neither of these explanations seems adequate to account for the results obtained. In some way not clearly explicable heat lessens nerve sensibility and abolishes pain. This remarkable thermic effect may be the result of inhibition acting through the temperature nerves of the skin. Whatever may be the explanation, we know that heat, properly applied, kills pain. This remarkable quality seems to be one of the specific properties of heat which it always possesses no matter what its origin. Heat waves of all lengths produce pain-relieving effects, but the luminous heat waves and the shorter infra-red rays found in the inner region of the infra-red section of the spectrum appear to be the most effective because of their greater penetrating power.

The specific effect of heat upon nerve sensibility is shown in its effect upon the tactile sense. Beginning with 113° F., tactile sensibility is steadily diminished as the temperature rises until at 130° F. it disappears entirely, the sensation at this point becoming pain.

Every person who has had any considerable experience in the use of heat for relief of pain has learned by observation that for decided effects the applications must be very hot, as hot as the patient is able to bear. Applications of lower temperature may give some relief and afford the patient considerable comfort, but to conquer the pain the application must be hot enough to produce on first contact with the skin a slightly painful sensation.

Heat Applications with Cooling Fan

The intensity of a hot application may be greatly increased by combining with it some means of simultaneously cooling the skin surface. This method requires the use of some suitable source of radiant heat. Either an arc light, the incandescent lamp or a heating element may be used. A small electric fan will supply the air current. With a current of air falling upon the heated surface the intensity of the light application may be doubled. This means that the tissues beneath the skin surface are receiving twice as large quantities of radiant energy as they could receive without the protective cooling of the skin surface. By this means quantities of heat may be applied which would be absolutely intolerable to the skin and would produce structural injury if long continued, and this without the slightest injury to the skin tissues or any interference with the passage of the penetrating heat rays to the deeper structures.

From the facts already stated it must be evident that cooling of the skin surface during an application of radiant heat is a matter of great practical importance. This is clearly shown by clinical experience. Cases in which no relief is obtained by ordinary hot applications readily yield to the massive doses of radiant energy which become permissible by this method. By moistening the surface from time to time so as to maintain evaporation in connection with the air current, the surface may be so efficiently cooled that the doses may be still further increased to three or four times the amount tolerable without the surface cooling. This method is especially applicable to cases of deep seated neuralgia such as chronic sciatica and in certain cases of visceral disease.

Intermittent Heat Applications

When it is desired to produce strong revulsive effects these may be readily attained by a slight modification of the method just described. By the use of a swinging electric fan the air current instead of being continuous will be interrupted at regular intervals. The light should be placed at such a distance from the skin that during the interruption of the air current the temperature will rise to the point of greatest tolerance. When the swing of the fan again causes the current to play upon the heated surface cooling will occur, to be followed by a quick rise as soon as the swing of the fan carries it out of range. The periods of heating and cooling may be doubled by placing the fan at right angles with the light and in such a position that when the side facing the patient is swung to the extreme limit the air current will still be felt. When this is done the patient receives the current while the fan is both going and coming or for the time required for one complete swing.

Another method of producing intermittent heating effects is by turning the current on or off at such intervals as may be desired. The switch controlling the current may be placed in the hands of the patient, who will regulate the duration of the application by counting. The heat should be so great that it can be tolerated only for a time not greater than that required for counting ten at a moderately rapid rate, say two counts to the second. Perhaps at first the point of tolerance may be reached at the end of five seconds. When the switch is turned off the patient counts ten while the skin is cooling then turns the current on and repeats the counting.

Instead of turning the current off and on by hand a mechanical or automatic interrupter may be employed. All of these different methods I have employed but find on the whole nothing better than the combination of the ordinary thermophore such as the Battle Creek Jr. Deep Therapy Lamp combined with the ordinary simple electric fan.

THE QUARTZ LIGHT

This well-known light appliance is mentioned last for the reason that for general purposes it is of least importance. Through the diligent effort of manufacturers, the quartz light or so-called mercury or arc lamp, has secured wide distribution and it is now found in most of the leading hospitals and in the offices of hundreds of private practitioners. Unfortunately, the mercury arc, which was held out by over-enthusiastic manufacturers as almost a panacea for nearly all human ills, as was to be expected, has signally failed to meet expectations.

The quartz light furnishes a large volume of light rays of short length but by no means represents the full therapeutic value of the sunlight, and to a still greater degree falls short of equaling the arc light in efficiency.

A large proportion of the rays of the water-cooled lamp are too short to be of value therapeutically, especially in general applications, and the infra-red rays are too long to be of value because of deficient penetrating power. As Coblentz has shown, the infra-red rays of greater length than 12,000 A. have little penetrating power.

Clinical experiences as well as theoretical consideration, have demonstrated the very great, if not preponderant, value of the visible, infra-red rays, not only because of their specific, individual value, but because of the superior results obtained in the use of ultra-violet when it is associated with luminous and infra-red rays, as in the sunlight and the light of the arc lamp.

That there is a difference in the quality of the light derived from the quartz lamp and the arc light is clearly shown in the difference in the character of the pigmentation produced. The pigmentation produced by a mercury lamp is bluish red; that caused by an arc light has a ruddy hue. Rays from the arc light are more penetrating and cause activity of the blood vessels and an increased movement of blood through the skin, whereas the effect of the quartz light is to cause a paralysis of the skin vessels and stasis of the blood as shown by the bluish coloration.

The quartz light steadily deteriorates because of changes which take place in the quartz and the accumulation of a deposit on the inside of the tube.

It cannot be denied that excellent results have been obtained by the use of the quartz light in the treatment of skin disorders of various sorts and even as the result of general applications in pulmonary tuberculosis, and especially in tuberculosis of the peritoneum; but these same results might have been obtained with the use of the arc light and probably in less time and with greater certainty.

A properly constructed arc lamp with electrodes capable of producing a strong, flaming arc, will produce as great a volume of ultra-violet rays as is furnished by an ordinary quartz light and much more than can be obtained from a quartz lamp that has been in use for any considerable length of time.

The arc lamp requires little more attention than the quartz, but rarely ever gets out of order; while the quartz lamp is so fragile that it is not only easily broken, but easily gets out of adjustment and at the best, steadily deteriorates from the moment it is set in operation.

A special use for the quartz lamp is in the treatment of skin lesions involving limited areas requiring an intensive application for destructive effects, and even in such cases the arc light may be employed with satisfactory results, by the aid of applicators adapted to the specific use required.

Unfavorable Reaction

Failure of patients to react to light treatment or unfavorable reaction, may be due to any or several of a number of causes, among which the following are the most common:

1. Too small dosage. This is probably the most common of the numerous causes of failure to obtain definite results from light treatment. The application must be sufficiently intense to produce a decided impression upon the major functions of the body. For maximum effect, a marked, though not excessive, erythema, must be produced.

Leonard Hill, working in conjunction with Sir Almroth Wright, found the bactericidal power of the blood increased "enormously after each treatment," when a decided erythema was produced.

In this country, so much publicity has been given to Rollier's cautions concerning over-dosage, with graphic descriptions of the terrible effects following intensive applications, that the almost universal tendency has been to over-caution. Much time has been wasted with trifling doses of light quite incapable of producing any appreciable reaction.

Uninformed newspaper writers have described sunburn or photo-erythema, in terms properly applicable only to heat burns, which are an altogether different lesion, unaware of the fact that the so-called "sunburn" is not a burn at all.

2. Too large dosage. Feeble and cachectic patients lack the power to react to large doses of light and are consequently endangered rather than benefited. The production of a pronounced erythema should not in itself be regarded as evidence of over-

dosage. Patients who are able to respond actively, are enormously benefited by the erythema dose, but feeble patients may be greatly depressed by a dose sufficient to produce a marked erythema.

3. A common cause of failure is neglect of the use of adjuvant measures, such as the cool air bath; the tepid or cool shower; proper diet, and especially proper attention to elimination, the functions of the colon and kidneys. The patient should be trained to evacuate the bowels after each meal by the use of a laxative diet and such dietary accessories as may be required.

In many cases, a daily enema is necessary at bedtime, especially in cases in which patients are confined to their beds.

Renal activity is promoted by copious water-drinking. At least three or four pints of water should be taken daily, in addition to the liquids taken at meals.

4. Unfavorable reaction may be due to an abnormal sensitivity to light. Persons who are subject to urticaria, who exhibit dermographism, when a pencil is drawn across the skin with pressure, are likely to react excessively even to small doses of light. On this account, a patient's susceptibility to light should be tested in every case before beginning treatment. It is to be remembered, also, that patients who have not previously given evidence of hypersensitiveness, may suddenly develop hypersensitivity as the result of the absorption through the food or otherwise, of any one of the various well-known sensitizers. Hematoporphyrin appears to be the most common cause in these cases.

Excessive reaction is especially likely to occur in persons who are hypersensitive to certain proteins and are subject to urticaria.

5. The depressing effect which patients often experience after a light application not of sufficient intensity to produce erythema, is usually the result of overheating. Warm baths are relaxing and produce a relaxing effect. This is rarely desirable in patients to whom light is applied and, as has been pointed out elsewhere in this work, should be prevented by cool or cold application immediately following a sun bath or light bath in which a heating effect has been produced.

Thermotherapy

Many years ago, the writer called attention to the fact that light is not a specific for any disease and should be used in conjunction with other measures which influence metabolism, especially thermic application. In the first edition of this work,* we wrote as follows:

"Phototherapy cannot be considered in itself a complete physiologic system for the reason that it offers no cooling procedure. Its effects are thermic and chemical, and in practice the two are generally combined.

"There are certain inconveniences accompanying all superheating procedures which must be compensated for if undesirable results are to be avoided. For example, it might be exceedingly disastrous to send out into the cold air of January a patient who has just emerged from an incandescent-light bath, or an application of the arc light to the back or any other large area. The cutaneous circulation is relaxed by hot applications, and its tone must be restored before the patient is released from the attendant's hands. Cool or cold water and cool air afford the most ready means of accomplishing this. Evaporating lotions may likewise be used.

"There are also certain depressant effects which follow and often accompany intense or prolonged applications of heat; these must be antagonized or compensated for by excitant or tonic applications of cold water or cold air.

"The combination of the eliminative, resolvent, derivative and inhibitory effects of phototherapy with the tonic, excitant and restorative effects which may be secured by suitable hydriatic measures, forms a most fortunate therapeutic partnership.

"Every physician who equips his office with the necessary appliances for the use of phototherapy should likewise equip his mind with information concerning the combined use of hydro-

---

*Light Therapeutics, Modern Medicine Pub. Co., 1912.

therapy with light applications, and should see that his office is supplied with facilities for at least the more simple hydriatic measures. These may be very few and inexpensive, or elaborate and comprehensive, as may suit the circumstances. Effective work can be done with a hand bowl and a towel, but there is always an opportunity for greater and better things. Phototherapy is a resourceful method and is daily accomplishing therapeutic wonders, but in the writer's view its greatest and most useful function is to introduce, and aid in establishing in modern medical practice, scientific hydrotherapy and the physiologic method."

It is unfortunate that writers upon phototherapy have in general presented light, if not as a panacea, at least as a specific curative agent. Under the dominance of this idea, almost exclusive attention has been given to such questions as sunlight, quality and intensity, as influenced by climatic conditions, etc.; lamp construction, dosage as regulated by the distance of lamp, duration of application, etc.; individual susceptibility, etc.

The same error has been made by the early promoters of nearly every one of the great therapeutic resources which constitute physiotherapy. The pioneers of hydrotherapy vaunted its theories as a cure for human ills and made use of it in a purely empirical manner.

Light therapy today is in much the same position as was hydrotherapy fifty years ago, before Schuteten, Fleury and Winternitz undertook to put it upon a sound scientific footing.

Gauvain, in a recent discussion before the Royal Society of Medicine, remarked (*Proc. Roy. Soc. Med., April, 1927*): "Heliotherapy in surgical tuberculosis is truly still more an art than an exact science."

Electrotherapy, like its predecessor, hydrotherapy, fell into disrepute because its promoters employed it to the exclusion of other remedies. Monotherapy succeeds only in exceptional cases. A rational therapy seeks to combine the use of therapeutic agents in such a way as to make the super-qualities of one make good the deficiencies of another and to counteract undesirable effects produced by one agent by the employment of another adapted to meet the particular indication.

Light therapy has made slow progress for the reason that it has been depended upon to meet all requirements. Leaders in phototherapy who have accomplished such great results at Leysin and Copenhagen, in their reports of the results of their remarkable experiences, have neglected to emphasize the important part played by air in connection with light treatment. This is perhaps due to the fact that at Lausanne, cold mountain air; and at Berck-Plage the cool waters of the English Channel, in which patients are dipped at certain seasons of the year, have incidentally played a more important part in the treatment and have contributed more largely to its success than has been appreciated.

In the writer's opinion, a great part of the benefit derived from treatment in Alpine resorts, is to be attributed to the cool, bracing air; and in seaside resorts, to the metabolic stimulation due to sea-bathing. Having from the beginning of his professional career given special attention to the development of a rational system of combined and co-ordinated physiotherapy in place of monotherapy which had been the bane of physiotherapeutics, the writer has always made use of light in connection with other measures, especially hydrotherapy, dietotherapy, open air treatment, exercises, etc. On this account, it is particularly gratifying to note a recent tendency among some of the leading exponents of light therapy, to recognize the principles set forth in the preceding paragraphs.

In a recent discussion on light treatment in surgical tuberculosis, before the Royal Society of Medicine, Sir Henry Gauvain calls attention to the seeming paradox that persons living in hot countries, even those tribes that wear little or no clothing, are, nevertheless, susceptible to tuberculosis.

Bernhard had previously called attention to the fact that children suffering from tuberculous glands which will not heal in high mountainous regions, in spite of the brilliant sunlight and direct radiation of the diseased parts, "rapidly improved at sea level or in brine baths in the plains."

Gauvain finds that when patients do not improve at Alton, the desired response to treatment is secured by a change to a seaside resort. He says, "The basal metabolism is enormously increased by sea-bathing, spraying, paddling, cool sea breezes and assistance given by the altered character of light. The different intensity of the light will not alone explain the change, the combination of altered stimuli will."

The same authority continues, "Continuous exposure to sunlight in the summer will not produce beneficial results nearly as speedily as alternations of light and shade, of heat and cold, of humid and dry air. Even the onset of a week or so of rainy or cloudy weather may be an advantage to the sun-cure in a hot summer."

The benefits which patients incidentally or casually receive from Alpine air, sea baths and weather changes, may be secured by judicious applications of hydriatic treatment and with beneficial results much more pronounced and far more dependable.

It is encouraging, also, to note that Levick and other intelligent and experienced clinicians devoted to light therapy, are beginning to make use of the douche and other hydriatic measures in connection with phototherapy.

Hundreds of practitioners who, through the reading of the works of Rollier and others, and especially through the persuasive influence of traveling manufacturers' agents, have invested hundreds of dollars in light appliances, have been disappointed in the results obtained, especially in the employment of light as a general measure in the treatment of pulmonary tuberculosis and other chronic disorders. Failure in many cases has been due, not to the inefficiency of the light appliance which may have produced a flood of light rays equal in intensity to those of the Alpine sun, but to the absence of the bracing Alpine air. Fortunately, this deficiency may be made good, so that results equal to those afforded by Rollier and other observers in Alpine regions, may be obtained by supplementing light treatment with thermic measures such as air baths and applications of water in various ways, as may be indicated in individual cases.

Both Gauvain of Alton and Reyn of the Finsen Institute invariably administer a cold or tepid douche after the general light bath (arc light). It has always been the practice of the author since he began the use of artificial light treatment in 1891, to

HYDROTHERAPEUTIC OR DOUCHE APPARATUS

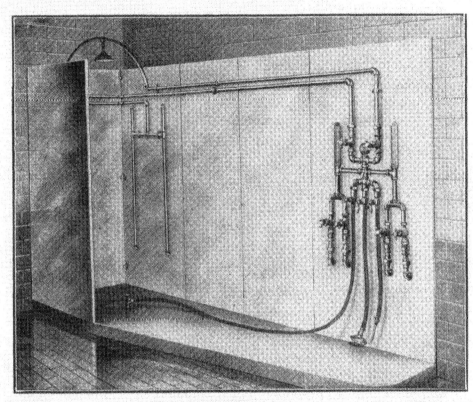

DOUCHE APPARATUS, SHOWING THE CONTROLLING AND REGULATING
MECHANISM

make after the light treatment a tonic, hydriatic application of some sort.

The principles involved in thermic applications of light are practically identical with those of thermic applications made by means of warm or hot water, hot air or steam. The limits of this volume will not permit a complete study of this subject, and the reader is earnestly urged to secure and study some one or more of the excellent treatises on hydrotherapy which may now be had. The author would especially commend the admirable books by Winternitz, Strasser, Buxbaum, Bottey and Beni-Barde. Baruch has the honor of being the first American to present a comprehensive treatise on this most vital subject. The author also desires to mention his own work, *Rational Hydrotherapy,* as a guide to hydriatic practice, and takes the liberty to borrow from this work several paragraphs and illustrative cuts descriptive of procedures which are of special service in connection with the application of phototherapy:

The Cold Douche

For a full discussion of the physiologic effects of the cold douche, and of its special indications and contraindications, see *Rational Hydrotherapy,* pages 426 to 522.

The accompanying cuts show the author's douche apparatus.

The jet douche consists of a single stream, varying in diameter from a millimeter or less (the filiform douche) to an inch or even more. The usual size is about three-eighths to half an inch. The horizontal jet is applied by means of a nozzle not unlike that of a garden hose, attached to a piece of rubber tubing two or three feet in length, so as to permit free movement.

In administering the horizontal jet, water may be employed at any temperature applicable to therapeutic purposes. The full force of the stream may be used where indicated, or the pressure may be broken, either by adjustment of the pressure-regulating valve or by breaking the force of the stream by placing the end of the finger in the stream near the mouth of the nozzle so as to scatter the column of water to the extent desired. The last-named means of lessening the pressure is always available, and must be used in all general applications in adapting the force of the stream to the different regions of the body.

The temperature of the *cold* douche is from 45° to 65°; of the *cool* douche, from 65° to 80°; of the *tepid* douche, from 80° to 92°; of the *neutral* douche, from 92° to 97°; of the warm douche, 97° to 104°; and of the *hot* douche, from 104° to 125°.

The employment of so vigorous a therapeutic procedure as the cold douche should always be conducted under the immediate supervision of an intelligent person who has been specially trained.

The *broken jet* is used over the heart and anterior portions of the chest; to the cervical region; and to all sensitive parts, as over the stomach, liver, bowels and uterus, in inflammation of these organs; *to inflamed or sensitive points; and over painful nerves.* The full jet, at appropriate pressure, may be used upon the back, arms, legs, feet, and over the liver and spleen when not contra-indicated.

The head must be very thoroughly cooled before the douche, and should be protected by a cold towel around the head or neck or both. The jet is usually first applied to the back for a few seconds, then the legs and arms, then over the anterior portions of the body and the liver, ending with a strong dash upon the feet. The whole body may be gone over several times in the manner suggested, each particular region being carefully respected as regards the appropriate degree of pressure, the patient turning around as directed by the attendant.

When the patient has previously been prepared for the cold douche by a heating process of some sort, which is generally the case, great care must be taken that he does not become chilled by exposure to the cooling effect of evaporation. To avoid this a cold procedure should follow the hot application instantly; or if a short interval must intervene, a few seconds perhaps, the patient must be protected by a warm woolen blanket. If there is the slightest cooling off by evaporation, causing chilliness, or if an interval of a minute or two has elapsed by reason of some emergency, the skin must be thoroughly warmed up again by a hot rain or needle douche before the cold jet is applied. The condition of the patient should be such that the cold water will not be regarded with extreme aversion and dread.

The Shallow Bath

In this procedure the patient is rubbed while sitting in a tub partially filled with water. The requisites are a tub with four or six inches of water of the proper temperature, a sheet, two or three towels, and a large dipper.

The patient, having been properly prepared,—the feet warm, the general circulation well established by exercise or previous warming in bed or by a warm bath, the head protected by a towel wet with water at 60°,—seats himself in the tub with the legs extended, and immediately begins vigorous rubbing of his arms, chest, and abdomen, while the attendant rubs the back and sides with both hands for 20 seconds, then dips water from the tub and dashes it upon the back for 10 seconds, then rubs 20 seconds; then the patient lies down in the bath while the attendant rubs his legs for 10 seconds. This occupies just one minute. For a two-minute bath, the above is repeated; for a bath of three minutes, the procedure is repeated a third time.

At intervals of one minute the patient should lie down in the bath, so that the whole body except the head is submerged for 5 to 10 seconds, the attendant rubbing the legs vigorously in the meantime.

When employed for tonic effects, the temperature of the water should be 75° to 65°, and the length of the bath 1 to 3 minutes. For the reduction of temperature in febrile cases, the temperature should be 85° to 70°, and the duration 6 to 15 minutes.

The depth of the water in the shallow bath is ordinarily not more than six inches; if deeper, it interferes with the rubbing.

The *standing shallow bath* is a modification of the bath in which the patient stands in a tub containing water at 75° to 80°. The patient is rubbed by two attendants, one on each side. The water is poured over his spine, chest, and shoulders, at intervals of 15 or 20 seconds. In rubbing the legs, the attendant's hands are constantly dipped in the water, and very vigorous friction is applied, duration 1 to 3 minutes.

At the conclusion of the bath, a pailful of cold water (60° to 55°) is poured over the patient, thus insuring good reaction. He is then quickly dried and vigorously rubbed, after which he should engage in moderate exercise until good reaction is secured.

The Salt Glow

In this procedure, salt of medium fineness and slightly moistened is applied to the surface of the body with friction movements, the amount of pressure being adjusted to the patient's sensation. With very thin-skinned persons, abrasion and irritation of the skin may be very easily produced. Persons of dark complexion, whose skins are usually thick, bear more vigorous applications than blondes.

The patient prepares for the treatment by lying down upon a slab or bed covered with a sheet, having previously been divested of his clothing. The sheet is drawn over the patient to prevent chilling. One part after another is then exposed and rubbed with the moistened salt, two or three pounds of which should be conveniently at hand in a basin. When this treatment is given in an institution, the patient may sit upon a stool, lie upon a slab, or stand upon a low stool, while receiving the application, in a room especially arranged for the purpose, and at a temperature sufficiently high to prevent chilling.

After the application, the salt which adheres to the surface is removed by the cold affusion, shower, or spray. The patient is quickly dried and rubbed in the usual manner. It will be noticed that the skin is hard and almost as smooth as marble after this application. In cases of feeble patients, a dash of hot water or a warm shower should be given just before the final cold application.

Cold Mitten Friction

By the term "cold friction" is designated a procedure which consists in the application to the surface of the body of a series of partial wet rubbings, one part after another being taken in systematic order until the whole cutaneous surface has been brought into vigorous reaction.

The requisites are: (1) A vessel containing a few quarts of cool, cold or very cold water; ice-water may be employed in many cases. (2) A mitt consisting of rough material of some sort,—ordinary rough linen or Turkish toweling is not desirable. Coarse mohair answers fairly well for the purpose; but the best fabric is a closely woven woolen cloth resembling hair-cloth but slightly rougher to the touch, which is manufactured in Egypt and Turkey, where the author became acquainted with it in the Turkish baths of Cairo and Constantinople. It is there used for a sort of preliminary shampooing applied after the sweating process is completed and before the application of soap. This material possesses just the right degree of roughness, stimulating the skin without irritating it, and is so closely woven that it may be made to hold just the right amount of water for the purpose for which it is designed. (3) A Turkish sheet and one or two towels are also required.

The patient is undressed, and lies upon a bed or a massage couch wrapped in a Turkish sheet. First of all, the head, face, and neck should be wet with cold water. If the hair is not wet (ladies often object to this), a napkin wet with cold water should be placed over the face. The vessel containing the cold water is placed at one side, near the head of the couch; the attendant places the mitt upon the right hand, and then uncovers a small portion of the patient's body, preferably the front of the trunk. He then dips the mitt into the cold water, and proceeds to rub the surface until reddened, redipping the mitt one or more times, covering the whole surface rapidly. Care should be taken to secure reaction in each part before proceeding to the next. Then with his left hand the attendant extends the arm and treats it in like manner, drying rapidly and covering. The other arm is then treated, and then in succession, the legs, and back of the hips, the back of the legs and, lastly, the feet. The soles of the feet should be spatted, not rubbed.

The Cold Towel Rub

This procedure consists in friction movements made upon a cold wet towel spread out upon the surface.

The requisites are a towel for the head, several linen towels for the application; a sheet and a towel for drying; a pail of water at the temperature desired for the application, and a basin of water at a temperature ten degrees lower.

The patient should lie in a recumbent position with all his clothing removed, and wrapped in a Turkish sheet and a woolen blanket, a portion of the covering being laid aside so as to expose the portion to which the application is to be made. The head, face, and neck are first bathed with the colder water, in which one of the towels is also wet, and wrapped about the head. A linen towel is then wrung very dry out of the water prepared for the purpose in the pail. After being quickly shaken out, it is applied smoothly to the part to be treated; and with the hands applied in such a manner as to cover as large a portion of the towel as possible, they are rapidly moved from point to point with firm pressure, so as to bring each part of the towel successively in close contact with the skin. The rubbing should be continued until the towel is warm, when it may be removed; the dry towel is then placed upon or wrapped about the part and it is rubbed until the skin is dry and *well reddened by reaction*. The corresponding part of the opposite side is then treated in like manner. If the patient is decidedly neurasthenic, special attention should be given to the back; while if the case is one of cardiac insufficiency, special attention should be given to the chest, arms, and legs.

The hands are rubbed upon the towel, but the towel is not rubbed upon the skin. Particular attention should be paid to this. The effect desired is not produced by mechanical irritation of the skin, but by the assistance rendered the circulation by the intermittent pressure upon the tissues. The hands are applied

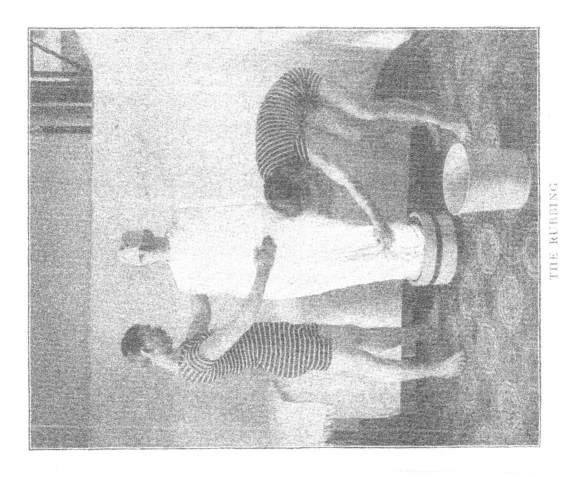

APPLICATION OF SHEET

THE RUBBING

THE WET SHEET RUB

with long, rapid, alternating strokes, falling upon the surface with sufficient force to give a decided percussion effect. The friction movements may be alternated every few seconds with gentle percussion. The whole surface of the towel should be gone over constantly, so as to avoid chilling by evaporation.

In order that the desired therapeutic effect may be obtained, the temperature of the water must be maintained at the initial temperature. This may be accomplished by employing a number of towels, so that no towel is used twice in the same application. A plan which the author prefers as more practical, however, is the following: Two pails or bowls of water are prepared, one of which is ten degrees lower than the temperature at which the application is to be made. The usual temperatures will be 60° and 50°. The face, neck, and head are cooled with the cooler water. After a towel has been applied to a surface and rubbed until warm, it is dropped into the cooler water, where it remains while the part is being dried and rubbed. In preparing the towel for a new application, it is gathered and squeezed, then dipped into the other pail (60°) and wrung out.

The Wet Sheet Rub

This procedure, perfected by Priessnitz, consists in a thorough rubbing of the body while enveloped in a wet sheet.

The requisites are a linen sheet, a Turkish sheet, two towels, a tub containing hot water for the feet, a pail of water at 60° to 70°. Water at a higher or lower temperature may be employed when indicated.

The patient, being prepared, the head cooled in the usual way and protected with a cold wet towel, stands in the tub of hot water with the dry sheet wrapped about him. The attendants prepare the wet sheet, which should be wrung dry enough so it will not drip rapidly.

When the sheet is ready, one assistant, holding one end of the linen sheet properly gathered in the right hand, and seizing the upper left-hand corner with his left hand, steps in front of the patient, while the other attendant withdraws the dry sheet and steps behind to assist. The patient holds up both arms, while the attendant in front places the upper left-hand corner of the sheet under his right arm; the patient then lowers the right arm, holding the sheet in place, while the attendant passes the sheet quickly across the front of the body beneath the left arm, which is then also lowered. The sheet is then carried around the body with the assistance of the attendant who stands behind the patient and pulls the bottom around. As the sheet is brought across the back of the patient, the attendant in front reaches over and seizes the upper edge of the sheet just above the point of the right shoulder, and pulls it first upward, then down upon the patient's chest, while with his other hand he carries the sheet across the chest, covering the fold, and over the left shoulder, deftly tucking the corner under the edge of the sheet behind.

The attendant behind tucks the sheet between the patient's legs, which are then brought tightly together. The sheet is thus brought everywhere in close contact with the skin. As soon as the patient is thus enveloped,—an operation which should be completed in 5 to 8 seconds,—both attendants begin to rub vigorously, covering the whole surface as quickly as possible, one, the legs and hips; the other, the trunk and arms. The rubbing should be continued for 1 to 3 minutes or until the sheet is everywhere thoroughly warmed. The attendants should bear in mind that *the patient is not to be rubbed with the sheet, but over the sheet, with downward percussion strokes.*

This is a most excellent procedure for concluding a vigorous electric-light bath, especially with obese patients and fleshy neurasthenics.

The Half-Sheet Rub

The half-sheet rub is one of the most convenient methods of cooling the skin after a general light bath when tonic effects are desired.

The requisites and preparation of the patient are the same as for the towel bath, except that a linen or cotton sheet is required instead of towels. The half-sheet or folded sheet is wrung dry out of water at room temperature, or 74° F. to 60° F., and is quickly and evenly spread over the patient's body from neck to ankles. The whole surface is then gone over rapidly with alternating long percussion strokes and vigorous clapping movements, until the sheet is well warmed. It is then thrown aside and the patient turns quickly over to undergo the same treatment on the other side. After the bath the patient is well dried and rubbed. The skin should be perfectly dry, smooth and warm before the patient is released.

The Cotton Poultice

This consists simply in the application to a part of a mass of dry cotton covered with mackintosh or other impervious material. The cotton is soon moistened by the retained perspiration, and thus the effect of a poultice is obtained, but in a much more cleanly and convenient manner. The cotton poultice is especially valuable in *chronic joint affections*.

Phototherapy with Air Bath

Cool air, if less versatile as a therapeutic agent, is equally as potent and efficient as cold water. On the whole, it is much more valuable and indispensable. Fortunately, it is the most available and least expensive of all therapeutic agents, at least during the cool season of the year, and during this period may be readily and inexpensively utilized as a most valuable adjuvant to phototherapy. No other apparatus than the ordinary electric fan is required.

The Cool Air Douche

This is a most convenient mode of applying cool air therapeutically. The temperature of the air must be 60° F., or less if possible, but need not be lower than 50° F. It is necessary that a strong air current should be used. This is essential to insure good and prompt reaction.

The air blast should be cold enough and forcible enough to make a decided stinging effect upon the skin. Reaction comes promptly, especially if the peripheral circulation is encouraged by rubbing of the skin by an attendant, or better, by the patient himself. The writer has for years made use of this means of cooling patients after the electric-light and other warm baths, and has seen no ill effects. It is a certain preventive of "taking cold" on going out after the bath.

For general cooling effects the patient stands before a strong electric fan and turns his body while rubbing himself until the skin is dry and cool, which requires usually not more than one or two minutes.

A better plan is to arrange four fans so as to concentrate the currents in the center of the space between them. The patient stands in the vortex of the currents, rubbing himself vigorously, and feels no uncomfortable sensation although being rapidly cooled by evaporation.

The Cabinet Air Bath

A most effective arrangement for obtaining the most pronounced effects is the cabinet air bath. The patient sits or stands in a small chamber or cabinet in which is a large fan or several small ones so placed as to expose the whole surface of the body to a strong current of cool or cold air. The purpose of the cabinet is to confine the cold air to the space necessary and thus prevent cooling of the adjacent room in which the patient is prepared for the bath.

This arrangement permits the employment of air at a temperature much lower than that of the ordinary room temperature. This is easily arranged in cold weather by a connection through a suitable conduit with the out-of-door air. In warm weather, the air may be cooled by means of ice or the evaporation of water.

The patient must dress and undress in a warm room. During the exposure the surface must be constantly rubbed either by the patient or by an attendant.

The duration of the bath will be 30 seconds to two minutes, according to the temperature of the air and the vigor and endurance of the patient. The bath should never continue so long as to produce a mottled appearance of the skin or pronounced chilliness.

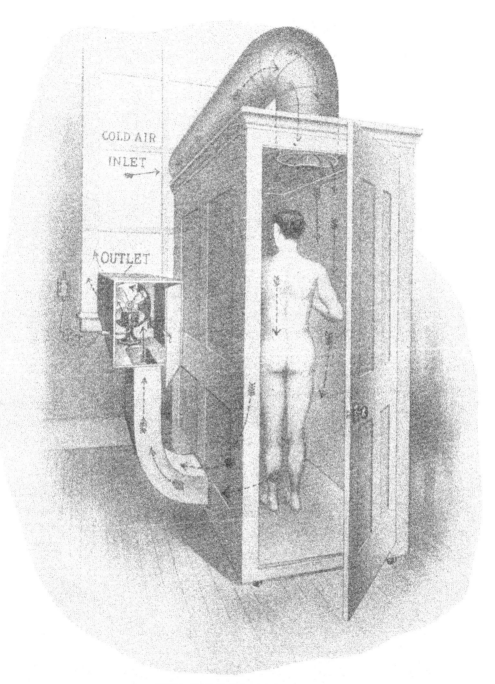

THE CABINET AIR BATH

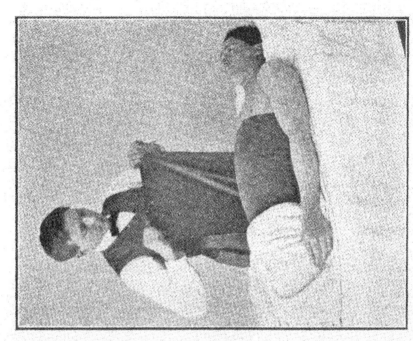

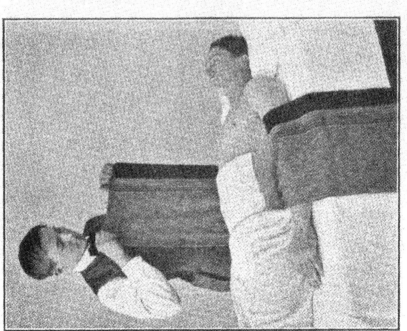

THE ABDOMINAL HEATING COMPRESS

The bath should be followed by massage or rubbing with oil in a warm room, to insure thorough reaction.

The patient may expose himself to the electric-light bath either before or after the air bath, or in alternation with it. Arc or incandescent lamps may be arranged in the cabinet.

The Light Bath With the Cardiac Compress

When the general surface is cooled during a light application, it is not necessary to give special attention to the heart, as the heart will profit by a tonic reflex from the entire surface of the body; but in general heating light applications, and in applications of the thermophore or the photophore to extensive areas, it is necessary to take the precaution to protect the heart by the cold precordial compress or an ice bag placed over the heart. In some cases it is also necessary to apply a cold application about the neck as protection for the brain.

The Arc Light or Photophore With the Heating Compress

When prolonged derivative or resolvent effects are required, as when the application is made for relief of deep visceral congestion or to stimulate the circulation through a deep-lying organ, as in cirrhosis of the liver, to relieve deep-seated pain or to stimulate absorption of chronic exudates from inflammation about a joint, chronic pelvic disease, pleuritic effusions and allied conditions, it is well to follow an application of the arc light or the photophore by the heating compress (See cuts). This is applied as follows: A towel or cheesecloth compress is wrung dry out of cold water (60° F. to 70° F.) This moist compress is applied to the skin. Then it is covered with a piece of mackintosh large enough to extend beyond the moist cloth an inch or two on all sides. Several thicknesses of flannel are then applied and bound tightly in place by means of a snug bandage. The purpose is to secure quick heating of the cool compress and retention of heat, so that the effect of a poultice is obtained.

The heating compress should be applied at once at the termination of the light application while the surface is still red and warm. The heating compress may be left in place for twelve to twenty-four hours. When it is removed the surface should be bathed with alcohol. The heating compress, once heated up, should not be allowed to become either cold or dry. At the first indications of cooling or dryness, the bandage should be removed. The good effects of the arc light or photophore are enormously increased by following the application with the heating compress.

Warming the Feet

In making general cold hydriatic applications, it is always necessary that the feet and legs should be well warmed so as to promote good reaction. If this precaution is neglected, headache and other disagreeable symptoms are likely to be induced and the good effects desired are not secured.

The photophore is one of the most excellent and convenient means of heating the feet and legs in preparation for a cold-mitten friction, a cold-towel rub, the salt glow, or any other similar tonic application. Its use is very much more convenient than the hot foot bath, especially in cases of bedridden patients.

For use in the wards of a hospital, it would be impossible to devise a more convenient method of warming the feet than the photophore. The great advantage of the photophore over the thermophore and other means of heating by contact is the fact that the heat rays penetrate the deep tissues and stimulate the heat-making processes of the tissues, whereas the effect of other means of heating is simply to warm the surface while at the same time reflexly inhibiting or depressing the heat-making functions of the parts to which the application is made.

Clinical Phototherapy

The experience gained in the employment of phototherapy in its varied forms at the Battle Creek Sanitarium, where this agent enters into the therapeutic program of eight or ten thousand patients yearly, with the published experiences of many hundreds of physicians who are now making regular use of phototherapy in hospital and private practice, affords ample ground for the statement that this agent must be classed among the great recent advances in modern therapeutics.

There is no other physical agent capable of producing more profound and beneficial effects than does light in assisting the body in its battle against chronic disease and degenerative processes. In cases of malnutrition, anemia, so-called nervous exhaustion, in patients convalescing from surgical operations, acute febrile disorders or other serious illnesses, it acts when properly applied as a powerful restorative measure. Its remarkable rejuvenating influence often produces results which seem almost magical. Not infrequently the patient experiences even during the application a sense of well-being and exhilaration which inspires faith and confidence and even enthusiasm, which are a powerful psychologic aid in promoting recovery.

The specific reactions due to light rays do not make their appearance for some hours after an application, but the thermic effects appear at once and should receive immediate attention. This is a point which seems to have been generally overlooked; but it is important and should receive due consideration. Every light application, except in the case of the quartz or mercury arc light, is also a heat application, and demands the same attention that should be given in connection with any other application of heat.

Fever Convalescence

The cabinet bath may be employed with great advantage in cases of convalescents from typhoid fever and other infectious fevers. It is one of the most effective means of combating the anemia and malnutrition resulting from the prolonged action of fever toxins upon the blood and tissues. The application must be short, and should be followed by short tonic, hydriatic applications, such as the mitten friction or towel rub.

Still more efficient is the general arc light, or sunshine bath, given in such a manner as to produce a first or second degree erythema. If the patient is quite feeble, the first exposure should be short, barely long enough to produce erythema of the first degree. In two days the time may be doubled. If a second degree erythema is produced, the application should be interrupted for two or three days until the reaction has largely disappeared.

The anemia which often follows scarlet fever, especially in cases in which the kidneys have been involved, is a condition to which light baths are particularly applicable. The arc light is in these cases preferable to the incandescent-light bath because of its more powerful influence upon the skin. The applications should be short, and should be made to cover the entire surface by successive seances until the whole skin has been gone over and is thoroughly tanned. The application should, of course, not begin until after the acute congestion produced by the disease has subsided, for Cnopf has shown that the ultra-violet rays are highly pernicious in scarlet fever. He believes, on the other hand, that the red rays are distinctly curative. As to these effects Cnopf says:

"The effect of the red light treatment of scarlet fever is twofold. The fever, which under ordinary treatment usually persists until the rash fades, falls, almost by crisis, and reaches normal in three or four days, instead of in seven or eight days, as is the case under ordinary treatment. The skin lesion is also markedly affected, the red color so characteristic of the disease gradually fading. The complications of the disease are apparently not affected, as in several cases secondary angina or pneumonia served to cause an increase in the fever as usual."

The indication in these cases is to increase immunity and build up vital resistance. This is best accomplished by the arc light bath administered in such a way as to produce a second degree erythema. If the patient is fairly strong the application may be made the first day to one side of the body and the next day to the other side. The purpose of this plan is to avoid giving the patient too great an amount of discomfort. If the patient is quite feeble, the area treated at the first application should not exceed one square foot or at most one and one-half square feet. The next day another area of equal extent is treated and so continuing from day to day until the whole surface of the body has received a second degree erythema dose. By this means, as shown by Eidinow, Leonard Hill and others, the immunizing properties of the blood may be increased to a marked degree.

Short applications of the electric-light cabinet followed by the very short cold douche or, in the case of fever patients, milder tonic applications, are most effective means of combating the cachexia which results from chronic malarial infection. The general light application should be short. As soon as the patient begins to perspire, he should be removed from the bath, and the cold application should follow immediately while the skin is still warm.

Cachexias Due to Toxemia

A large share of the maladies formerly attributed to uric acid are now known to be due to the disturbing influence of subtle poisons generated in the intestine and absorbed into the blood. So long as the body is able to oxidize and destroy these poisons or eliminate them, no unpleasant symptoms appear; but sooner or later the power to oxidize and eliminate them is diminished, the tissues become saturated with toxins and most profound disturbances are produced.

Experience shows that the general application of light either by means of the electric-light cabinet or the arc light, is extremely useful in promoting recovery. In this whole class of disorders, as pointed out years ago by Bouchard in his interesting volume, *Renseignement de la Nutrition,* there is slowed metabolism, decreased oxidation, deficient elimination of waste matters, and depreciation of the blood and tissues in general. The effect of retention of these poisons is to produce spasm of the surface vessels with resulting visceral congestion.

General Light Applications are of greatest value in relieving all these conditions. Under the influence of the thermic rays of the electric-light bath, the general surface vessels are relaxed, thus relieving visceral congestion. By repeated applications of the arc light, this relaxation of the surface vessels and the improved circulation through the skin may be rendered permanent. The arc light applications should be made daily or in alternation with the cabinet bath, and the entire surface should be gone over in successive applications until the skin is well reddened.

The arc light, the photophore and the thermophore render the greatest service also as measures of relief and cure in neuralgia, myalgia, arthropathies and various other painful and disabling local affections which are encountered in this class of disorders. In general, these local applications should be made daily. The duration should be from five to twenty minutes. The effects may be greatly enhanced by the application of a heating compress after the light application.

It must be remembered, of course, that these applications, whether general or local, deal only with the symptoms and results of the disease, and do not affect the cause, which must be sought out and removed. These patients should always be advised to live outdoors as much as possible, to arrange outdoor sleeping rooms, or at least to sleep with the windows wide open at all seasons. Most of all it is important that the patient should be instructed to adopt an antitoxic dietary and to make use of yogurt. Intestinal activity must be increased to the extent of securing at least two thorough evacuations daily. This may be best accomplished by means of the use of laxative foods. It is of the highest importance in these cases that the intestinal flora should be changed so as to suppress intestinal putrefactions.

Diabetes

While insulin and careful regulation of the diet are the main factors in dealing with cases of diabetes, every other measure calculated to build up the patient's resistance and to encourage metabolism may be and when possible, should be, employed. Among such measures, none is more capable of rendering substantial service than light treatment skilfully applied. Light baths accelerate metabolism.

If the cabinet is used, the patient should lie half the time upon the face so that the great muscular masses of the back and thighs may be brought fully under the influence of the thermic rays. In employing the arc light, the application should be made as intense as the patient can endure. The whole surface of the body should be exposed to the influence of the rays in successive applications. About half the surface should be gone over at each seance.

Light applications in diabetes should be made daily, and the duration should be fifteen to thirty minutes. Strong patients may receive two applications daily. There is credible data for believing that under the influence of the electric-light bath, sugar oxidation may be increased.

It is especially important in this disease to avoid the depressing effects of overheating the skin; hence the skin surface should be cooled during the bath by the electric fan or other means, as has been pointed out elsewhere.

The good effects of the light bath in diabetes may be greatly enhanced by a prolonged tepid or cool bath immediately following. Patients of ordinary strength may with great advantage spend fifteen to thirty minutes in the swimming pool. Both the exercise and the low temperature of the water are effective means of stimulating oxidation and hence encourage the combustion of sugar in the tissues. In the absence of the swimming bath, an ordinary shallow bath may render effective service. The bath is administered in an ordinary bathtub. The temperature of the water should be about 80°. After a little training, a lower temperature may be employed. The patient sits in the bathtub and rubs his legs vigorously with both hands at frequent intervals, dashing the water up around the trunk and arms, and rubbing these parts. The rubbing should be sufficiently vigorous to prevent chilling of the surface or the appearance of goose-flesh. The patient may work as hard in the bathtub as in a swimming pool, and thus may get the same benefit, although in a less agreeable manner. The whole body should be submerged in the bath with the exception of the head, so as to produce a strong tonic effect upon the entire surface. The rubbing should be continued during the submergence.

If the patient is not strong enough to rub himself with sufficient vigor, he should be rubbed by an attendant. The services of an attendant are always advantageous.

Obesity

Light baths may render service in all forms of obesity. For rapid results, the light cabinet may be used daily or even twice a day. The bath should be sufficiently prolonged to cause the loss of one or two pounds of weight in perspiration.

After the bath, the patient should be well cooled by a prolonged shower bath at about 80° F., ending with a douche at 60° F., or less. Swimming in a pool, with the water at a temperature of 78° or 80° F., is most advantageous. The patient should of course exercise as much as his strength will permit, and the diet should be greatly restricted.

In cases of endocrine disturbance, thyroid and pituitrin are required. Obese persons who suffer from rheumatism to such a degree that exercises are difficult, are particularly appropriate subjects for light treatment. Light baths are especially valuable in these cases because the radiant energy penetrates to the muscles and stimulates their development. This beneficial factor is not obtained from the Turkish, vapor, hot air bath or any other form of heating. Because of this peculiar property, the light bath to some degree takes the place of muscular exercise, a precious resource in cases in which the patient is unable to take exercise in the ordinary way.

The arc light may be used for producing general, eliminative effects by applying it in succession to different parts of the body, but it renders greater service in local applications to parts which are the special seat of excessive fat accumulation, as the buttocks, the breasts and the shoulders.

The arc light also renders great service applied in an intensive manner to the joints when painful, as is often the case in obese patients. In this local use of the arc light, it is desirable to make an application sufficiently intense and prolonged to produce a decided erythema.

Whenever possible, automatic exercises should be employed in connection with light treatment in cases of obesity. This form of exercise is practically indispensable in the treatment of patients who because of joint affections or heart weakness, are unable to take ordinary exercise.

Careful attention to diet is also essential. The intake of fats and carbohydrates should be reduced two-thirds or one-half. Care should be taken to avoid lessening the intake of salts and vitamins. Roughage should be freely used. The diet should be made largely to consist of greens, coarse vegetables and fresh fruits.

Those who desire more detailed information on the feeding of obese cases are referred to the author's work, "The New Dietetics."*

The cabinet bath should be short, and should not be allowed to continue after the patient begins to perspire, and at the beginning should stop short of perspiration. As soon as the skin is well heated, the patient should be removed from the bath, and a very short cold application should be made. The mitten friction, the cold-towel rub, the salt glow or a half-sheet rub are the most effective means. It must not be forgotten that this disease is one of malnutrition and hence requires proper regulatioin of diet. Flesh meats of all sorts should be excluded. The diet should be strictly antitoxic. It is especially important that the patient have

---

The New Dietetics. By Dr. John Harvey Kellogg. Modern Medicine Publishing Co.

an ample supply of raw food, such as yogurt buttermilk, orange juice, fresh apple juice, lemon juice and, when the digestive organs will permit, raw celery, lettuce, and raw fruits of all sorts. Ripe bananas prepared by rubbing through a colander are excellent in these cases.

Special attention must be given to the bowels, which in these cases swarm with putrefactive organisms. Active peristaltic activity should be assured by a laxative and antitoxic diet.

Anemia

As shown elsewhere in this work, light treatment is of the greatest service as a means of aiding blood regeneration. The influence of light upon the blood in increasing immunizing power is one of its most notable effects. A thorough course of light treatment is indicated in every case of anemia, secondary or primary.

Sun baths are best, because of the tonic influence of the open air; but Kestner noted very marked effects from the arc light.

At the start of treatment, a first or second degree erythema should be produced. After omitting treatment for two or three days, the exposures should be made daily, and continued until the skin is deeply tanned.

Care must be taken to avoid overheating the patient, and each treatment should be terminated by a cool shower or towel rub. Great care must be given the diet to insure an abundant intake of food iron by the free use of greens, and whole grain cereals. Savita and Food Ferrin are dependable sources of iron which render good service when a large intake of this element is needed.

Chlorosis

Employed in connection with careful feeding and tonic baths, general radiation either by sun bathing or the arc light, secures excellent results in cases of chlorosis. But instead of making general applications at first, the treatment should be confined to limited areas. The first day, legs and front and back; the second day, the back; the third day, the anterior portion of the trunk.

These patients are likely to react badly, but by these precautions unpleasant effects may be avoided. It is important to keep in mind that these patients are rather likely to be hypersensitive.

By skilful handling, the regenerative effects of the sunlight soon become apparent in these cases and the patients often make rapid improvement.

Exophthalmic Goiter

Light treatment gives much satisfaction in goiter cases when employed in connection with other treatment commonly used in the treatment of this disease. By the suppression of toxic-forming foods and careful restriction of the patient to a basic, antitoxic diet in connection with general radiation daily or every other day, and rest, these cases may often make a recovery without surgical intervention even when surgery may seem to be decidedly indicated. The time required is often long and the physician as well as the patient may be severely taxed, but recovery may be secured in so many cases, it seems quite worth while to inquire whether in the sacrifice of the thyroid gland, there may not be a risk of imperiling the welfare of the body in later years. The thyroid naturally shrivels with advancing years and it is reasonable to suppose that when a portion of thyroid has been removed, the period of thyroid insufficiency will arrive earlier than when the organ is retained intact.

Hyperacidity

Prolonged electric-light cabinet baths are of great service in this condition. The bath should be applied in such a way as to produce vigorous perspiration. The best time for the bath is an hour before eating, or soon after eating. By producing marked hyperemia of the skin and especially by removing a large amount of chlorid of sodium, the secretion of hydrochloric acid is diminished. The pain often present in this condition may be relieved by the application of the arc light or the photophore to the spine and the epigastric region. A second degree erythema should be produced over the epigastrium covering an area of 10 or 12 inches in diameter and a similar area of erythema should be produced upon the back opposite.

The diet should be strictly antitoxic. Flesh foods and animal broths and extracts must be absolutely forbidden because of their exciting effect upon the gastric mucous membrane, as shown by Pavlov.

Peptic Ulcer

Ulcer of the stomach or duodeum of course requires special dietetic treatment and often surgery. The arc light and the photophore may render valuable service as a means of relieving the pain which in these cases is sometimes agonizing. The application should be made both anteriorly and posteriorly. Second or third degree erythema should be produced. The application of the arc light may be renewed after five or six days. The photophore employed intensively may be used daily. General light baths should be given, both arc light and incandescent.

When the ulcer is penetrating, as shown by the X-ray, an operation is required.

In other cases a cure may often be effected by a combination of dietetic measures with local and general light treatment. Prompt relief often follows the use of Lacto-Dextrin in such a manner as to change the intestinal flora. A dose of Lacto-Dextrin will usually produce immediate relief from the severe gastric pain due to pyloric spasm. It apparently acts by stimulating the flow of alkaline diluting juice produced in the pyloric region of the stomach.

Chronic Gall-Bladder Disease

This condition is present in about half the cases of so-called indigestion accompanied by pain in the right hypochondriac region and the epigastrium. When a positive Graham test or other indications point definitely to a diseased condition of the gall bladder, an operation is usually required; but there are undoubtedly many cases in which the natural curative powers of the body may be able to correct the conditions present. In such cases the intensive application of the photophore once or twice daily or a second degree erythema dose of the arc light will greatly assist the curative process.

Gastric Pains

The photophore renders great service in these cases as a very convenient means for the intensive application of heat. A cooling air current should be used in connection with the photophore. Applications may be made whenever pain is experienced.

It is of course necessary to give attention to the removal of the causes of these pains. A diseased gall bladder, either with or without gallstones or a diseased appendix, must be removed. Penetrating gastric ulcers require surgical interference. Superficial gastric or duodenal ulcers may often be made to recover quickly by tube-feeding and other suitable dietetic measures. Lacto-Dextrin renders valuable service in these cases by changing the intestinal flora not only of the colon but also the duodenum and other portions of the upper alimentary tract.

Ulcer of the stomach or duodenum is a pathological process due to bacterial infection just as is an ulcer of the rectum, colon or the skin or any other structure. When the pathogenic bacteria which are the immediate cause of the destructive process are destroyed or rendered inactive, the damaged parts are quickly repaired and thus a cure is accomplished. Lacto-Dextrin or lactose administered in these cases is beneficial not only in preventing the growth of pathogenic bacteria and thus combating the immediate cause of the ulceration but also by reducing the acidity of the gastric juice and thus lessening the spasm of the pyloric sphincter, and so relieving pain. This beneficial result is due to stimulation of the glands of the pyloric portion of the stomach which secrete an alkaline diluting juice. A dose of Lacto-Dextrin will produce almost immediate relief from the pain due to pyloric spasm which is often experienced in these cases either soon after eating or three or four hours later when the stomach is nearly emptied, and the continued use of this product with care to keep the colon free from accumulated and putrefying food residues, will often effect a cure even in cases in which other measures have failed and thus save the necessity for surgical interference.

Cirrhosis of the Liver

This condition is of course incurable, but it may be greatly mitigated by the use of general applications of the arc light or the cabinet bath two or three times a week, and the arc light over the region of the liver and the abdomen with sufficient intensity to produce a decided hyperemia.

In cases of chronic cirrhosis of the liver, with or without abdominal dropsy, applications may be made with benefit. In these cases an antitoxic diet with change of the intestinal flora and the regulation of the diet in such a manner as to secure full evacuation of the colon at least three times a day, will render great service. In these cases meat should be wholly discarded from the dietary, together with tea and coffee. The use of laxatives and other drugs should be avoided. Every effort should be made to lighten the burden of the liver as much as possible.

Indigestion

The pains in the region of the stomach occurring soon after eating may be due to gastric ulcer, disease of the gall bladder, pancreatic disease, disease of the duodenum and lesions of other portions of the intestinal tract. For permanent relief, of course, it is necessary that the cause should be removed. Temporary relief may often be obtained, whatever may be the cause, by the application of a third degree erythema dose of arc light over the upper abdomen and upon the back opposite. The treatment should cover an area at least 10 or 12 inches in diameter. Change of the intestinal flora and regulation of the diet is of course necessary.

Colitis

Light treatment is by no means a specific remedy for colitis, but that it may render great service in the treatment of this disorder, the writer has seen demonstrated in multitudes of cases. Neither sun baths nor arc-light baths will render dietetic measures unnecessary, but used in connection with a proper regimen, general and local light application render great service. It is to be remembered that colitis is simply an infection of the colon, the natural result of the free use of flesh foods and the lack of roughage in the dietary, which leads to constipation. The colon is constantly filled with highly putrefactive residues. As a matter of fact, meats are generally eaten in a state of fairly well advanced putrefaction. As Tissier has shown, these putrefactive bacteria are the cause of colitis.

One of the consequences of this disease is a spastic condition of the colon, which often gives rise to pain and misery not only in the abdominal region but in the back. Reflex pains not infrequently extend into the legs and the effects are experienced in remote parts of the body, manifested in pains in the joints and muscles, often accompanied by stiffness and swelling and various other disturbances such as biliousness, loss of appetite, so-called nervous exhaustion and a great variety of chronic ailments.

The usual treatment of this disease is quite unsatisfactory and many physicians have on this account come to regard colitis as incurable. This, however, is an error except in cases in which the disease has advanced so far as to involve to a great extent all the structures of the intestinal wall as well as the mucous membrane.

The measures essential for success in the treatment of colitis are a radical change of diet in the adoption of an antitoxic regimen, discarding meat and eggs, the use of liberal quantities of roughage and laxative accessories such as Fig Bran, agar, paraffin oil and psyllium seed and the use of efficient means for changing the intestinal flora such as lactose or Lacto-Dextrin. It is highly important also to cleanse the colon thoroughly at least once a day by washing it out with water at a temperature of 115° to 120° F. The quantity usually required is about two quarts. It is frequently necessary to repeat the enema several times before the colon is completely emptied.

Used in connection with these measures the arc light may render very great service. It should be applied to the abdominal wall in such a way as to produce the third degree erythema. This should be repeated from five to seven days. It will of course be necessary to increase the dosage in order to produce the effect desired. A repetition of the erythema should be secured as many times as possible. In some cases it may be necessary to interrupt the light applications for as long a period as ten days or two weeks to give the skin an opportunity to recover its sensitivity to light. General arc light applications may be used with advantage as a means of improving general resistance. The open air treatment is also highly valuable for the same reason.

Neuritis

Neuritis, from whatever cause, may generally be greatly relieved by light applications. The penetrating thermic rays afford relief from pain when other measures fail, and thus obviate the necessity for the use of opium and other pain-relieving drugs, which generally leads to most disastrous results in chronic cases of this sort as well as in other forms of chronic pain. The arc light and the photophore are the most effective measures. General light applications may be made several times a week with advantage as a means of improving the general nutrition. The intestinal toxemia which is a most common cause of this condition must be combated by an antitoxic diet, and by securing thorough and regular evacuation of the bowels three times a day. This must be accomplished by the use of a laxative and antitoxic diet. Flesh foods and condiments should be excluded from the dietary.

In cases of chronic sciatica, a marked second degree erythema should be produced over the lower part of the back and the whole length of the limb over the course of the sciatic nerve. Each application should be followed by another within a week or as soon as the reaction from the previous application has mostly disappeared.

After local applications for the relief of neuritis, it is generally best to apply the heating compress so as to continue the beneficial effects secured.

In obstinate cases light treatment may be advantageously supplemented by applications of diathermy.

Neuralgia

The same measures as have been recommended above for neuritis may be employed with equal success in neuralgia. In chronic cases, a strong hyperemia of the skin should be produced over the affected part in cases in which the pain does not readily yield to milder applications.

Chronic Myelitis and Spinal Sclerosis

It is of course too much to expect a radical cure of organic disorders of the spinal cord, but light applications are certainly effective in greatly mitigating the condition of these patients. In most cases a judicious employment of light baths in connection with hydrotherapy, regulation of diet and other hygienic measures, will be found effective in arresting the disease. Not infrequently a very considerable degree of improvement can be secured. In patients who are fairly strong, the electric-light cabinet bath should be employed at least two or three times a week in such a manner as to secure vigorous perspiration, after which the tonic cold application should be made, such as the wet sheet rub, the cold mitten friction or the salt glow. The arc light may be applied to the spine with great advantage. A cooling measure should be used at the same time so that the application may be made as intense as possible. Excellent derivative effects may be secured by producing decided erythema of the skin. The antitoxic diet should be employed in connection with yogurt tablets and whatever measures may be needed to secure free intestinal activity. This is very essential for the reason that there is considerable ground for believing that many organic affections of the spine are the result of the absorption of toxins from the alimentary canal; hence it is important that the food remnants should be hurried through the intestine at such a rate that there will not be time for putrefaction to take place.

Locomotor Ataxia

Much more can be done for this disease than is generally supposed. General light applications two or three times a week, and especially the arc light to the spine daily, are measures of value. The arc light applied to the spine and over the areas subject to lightning pains, is a good means of relieving this most distressing symptom. Combined with proper diet, educative gymnastics, and thorough specific treatment, phototherapy may assist in arresting the disease and causing the disappearance of its characteristic symptoms. The lost reflexes will not return, but sufficient co-ordination may be secured to greatly improve the gait.

Epilepsy

This disease is by no means so hopeless as it has been commonly regarded to be. Phototherapy combined with an outdoor life, hydrotherapy, and a strict dietary will accomplish wonders in some of these cases. A vigorous application of the general light bath should be made at least three times weekly. The patient should sweat profusely. After the bath, a vigorous cooling application of some sort should be made. The arc light may be applied to the spine on alternate days. The patient should strictly follow an antitoxic diet, excluding flesh meats of all kinds. It is important to eliminate salt from the dietary. In some cases this régime, combined with proper medication, will cause the prompt and complete disappearance of the paroxysms.

Hysteria

All but the most inveterate and degenerative cases will yield to the persevering application of phototherapy and appropriate hydriatic measures. The patient must, of course, be required to comply with all the rules of hygiene in relation to diet, sleep, etc. Short electric-light cabinet baths may be employed two or three times a week. The arc light should be applied to the spine on the alternate days. Local paralyses are relieved by the arc light or the photophore followed by rubbing. Both sensory and motor paralyses often yield very promptly to these measures. Contractions require prolonged applications of the photophore followed by cold rubbing and massage. Hyperesthesias and paresthesias are relieved by the arc light with the red screen or the photophore. Visceral neuralgias yield to the arc light and the photophore followed by the heating compress. Spinal irritation is best relieved by the application of the arc light in such a way as to produce a decided erythema.

Neurasthenia

The profound effects of light upon the mind and nervous system render this one of the most efficient of all means of combating this condition in which psychic as well as physical factors must be dealt with. As illustrative of the mental influence of light we quote the following account of the celebrated French author, M. le Sage, when a very old man:

"M. le Sage awakened every morning as soon as the sun appeared some degrees above the horizon, became animated, acquired feeling and force in proportion as that planet approached the meridian; but as the sun began to decline, the sensibility of the old man, the light of his intellect, and the activity of his bodily organs began to diminish in proportion, and no sooner had the sun descended some degrees under the horizon than he sank into a lethargy from which it was difficult to rouse him."

In the treatment of neurasthenics the best results are obtained from sun baths in the open air or the open air use of the arc light. In the use of the arc light heating effects should be avoided. When the bath is given indoors a fan should be used to keep the skin cool. In very feeble patients the duration of the bath should be such as to produce an erythema of the first degree, but in stronger patients the duration of the application should be sufficient to produce a second degree or even a third degree erythema. Each application should be followed by another one of increased intensity as soon as the reaction has subsided.

The neuralgias often present in this condition are relieved by local applications of the arc light or the photophore or the thermophore, followed, if necessary, by a cotton pack.

The paresthesias, aches and other miseries which often accompany this condition usually disappear after a few general light applications. The diet should be strictly antitoxic and the intestinal flora should be changed and kept changed. Attention to diet and keeping the colon free from putrefying residues are measures of first importance.

The electric-light cabinet may be used two or three times a week with advantage. It should always be followed by careful cooling of the skin by means of the cold-mitten friction, cool shower or the neutral bath. The arc light may be advantageously used in these cases as a means of overcoming the spasm of the vessels of the skin which nearly always exists. Applications of sufficient intensity to produce erythema of the second degree may be made over the entire body at successive seances. It is most gratifying in these cases to see how great improvement may be secured by a proper regulation of the dietary in combination with electric-light baths.

Migraine

This disease is generally due to intestinal autointoxication in combination with a special susceptibility or predisposition of the nervous system. Intestinal autointoxication must be combated by an antitoxic diet, discarding flesh foods entirely, and especially by stimulating intestinal activity and changing the intestinal flora.

There is generally a foul condition of the tongue, and putrid stools are usually encountered in these cases. No permanent relief can be obtained until these conditions are removed. Tonic applications of the electric-light bath may be made two or three times a week. The arc light may be applied to the spine on alternate days.

General arc light baths applied in such a way as to produce a second degree erythema are highly beneficial as also are arc light applications to the abdomen. Such applications are highly useful in combating the colitis commonly present and relaxing the spastic colon, which often hinders proper elimination.

These cases are benefited, but never cured by light treatment only. The elimination of meat and eggs and in some cases milk and eggs also, and change of the intestinal flora by the free use of Lacto-Dextrin, psyllium seed and roughage, are other measures necessary to success. Tea and coffee must be discarded, together with narcotics and stimulants of all sorts. An enema at bedtime (two quarts, temperature 115° F.) is often needed to insure complete elimination.

Chronic Bronchitis

This condition is often symptomatic of chronic toxemia or emphysema. It is always associated with lowered vital resistance. As general tonic measures, applications of light should be made at least three or four times a week, and care should be taken after the bath to cool the patient off properly. The application of the arc light to the back and the chest is a most effective means of relieving cough and expectoration. The application should be made of sufficient intensity and duration to produce decided erythema.

In chronic bronchitis accompanied by asthma marked relief is often obtained by inducing a second degree erythema of the chest with the arc light. An area 10 or 12 inches in diameter both in front and behind should be produced with the arc light and reproduced as soon as the symptoms of reaction wane.

The relief afforded by suitable applications of light in cases of bronchial asthma is often most gratifying. In addition to general arc light applications of such intensity as to produce a mild erythema of the skin with slight peeling, third degree applications should be made over the chest. The more pronounced the erythema, the greater will be the relief produced. The whole front of the chest should be thus treated at one application and two or three days later a similar application should be made to the upper part of the back.

In addition to these light applications careful attention should be given to the patient's diet. The flora should be changed and an antitoxic diet should be closely followed. This requires the exclusion of meat and eggs from the bill of fare. Roughage and laxative food accessories should be used systematically so as to secure three or four bowel movements daily. When the colitis and intense autointoxication usually present in these cases have disappeared, the patient will find himself permanently relieved of his bronchial troubles.

In many cases of bronchial asthma the patient is sensitized to some particular article of food, to house dust or some other specific substance. By means of the well-known sensitivity tests the disturbing causes should be discovered and the necessary measures taken for their removal.

Chronic Pleurisy

General tonic applications of the electric-light bath should be made together with local applications of the arc light, the photophore, or the thermophore. The arc light and the thermophore are the most effective means because of the penetrating character of the thermic rays. General cold frictions should be employed as a means of increasing vital resistance, and a heating compress should be applied over the chest. When the pain is in the front part of the chest, the arc light should be applied not only over the affected area, but over the whole chest surface, reaching as low as the umbilicus.

Pleuritic Pains

Pains in the chest due to chronic adhesions are usually relieved by an application of the arc light in such a way as to produce a third degree erythema. The application should be made over the seat of pain and should cover an area of 10 or 12 inches in diameter.

Melancholia

This condition is doubtless due in most cases to chronic toxemia; hence attention must be given to the dietary. It is of special importance that flesh meats should be excluded. Antitoxic foods only should be employed. Buttermilk may be used freely, especially yogurt buttermilk. The free use of prunes is advantageous. Special care should be taken to render the diet as laxative as possible.

The electric-light bath prolonged to the extent of producing vigorous perspiration should be employed two or three times a week. Applications of the arc light to the spine are extremely useful. Tanning the whole surface of the body by means of the arc light will be an excellent means of improving the patient's general vital condition. The portal circulation, which is always sluggish in these cases, may be encouraged by the application of the arc light or of the photophore to the abdomen, followed by ice rubbing and the wet girdle worn at night.

Since the above paragraphs were written, light treatment has been introduced into several state hospitals for the insane and with such excellent results that it is likely to be added to the therapeutic program of other hospitals of this class throughout the country.

Facilities for the use of the sun bath and light baths of various sorts should constitute a part of the equipment of every hospital. These methods are especially adapted to the treatment of mental cases because of simplicity of technic and convenience.

Habit Chorea

In addition to proper diet, gymnastic training and tonic hydrotherapy, the patient should be kept in the open air as nearly the entire twenty-four hours as possible. Besides sleeping in fresh air, the patient, dressed in small clothes, should be freely exposed to sun and air during the daytime when the weather is warm enough to permit. If the treatment begins in July or August, when the sun's rays are most intense, the first exposures should be of short duration, just long enough to produce reddening of the skin; but the patient should be kept in contact with fresh air in the shade and in such a position as to receive the skyshine; that is, the light reflected from the sky or bright clouds. As the skin becomes more and more pigmented, there is almost invariably a marked increase in physical vigor and gradually the patient's vital resources are improved to such a degree that a strong restorative effort is set up and definite and highly gratifying results are usually attained. When sun baths are not available, the arc light should be used instead.

Insomnia

A short electric-light bath, followed by a neutral bath for half an hour or the neutral spray for three or four minutes, is a most effective means of relieving insomnia.

No drugs should be given. The patient should be placed on a low protein diet. The stools should be examined and if B. Welchii is found present, the flora must be changed at once, and kept changed. An enema at bedtime is often greatly helpful in securing sleep.

Myxedema

Vigorous application of the electric-light cabinet bath should be made at least three times a week. Profuse perspiration should be induced. There is decided slowing of all the metabolic processes of the body in this condition, and diminished oxidation. A daily application of the electric-light bath may be made if care is taken to employ proper cooling measures such as the tepid or neutral shower.

The general arc light should be applied in such a way as to produce erythema of the second degree. The second application should be made after an interval of one day, after which the application may be renewed daily. Each general application of light should be followed by a vigorous cold application, such as the cold-towel rub or the half-sheet rub.

Diseases of the Bones and Joints

Both general and local applications of light are indispensable in the treatment of affections of the bony skeleton and its articulations. The dominating influence of light in controlling the metabolism of calcium and phosphorus has been demonstrated by Hess and other competent observers. The ultra-violet rays have been shown by Hess, Steenbock and others to be capable of effecting a cure of rickets resulting from a diet deficient in vitamin D without changing the diet. Exposure for a few minutes only was found quite sufficient to counteract the effect of the vitamin deficiency. Clinical observations by Percy, Hamilton, Rollier and others have clearly demonstrated the value of sunlight in promoting recovery from bone lesions whether due to traumatism or infection. The writer saw at Leysin, Switzerland, and at Berck-Plage, France, hundreds of cases of chronic joint and bone disease of a most advanced and aggravated character that were making admirable progress toward recovery, and scores of cases were seen in which recovery from apparently hopeless conditions was apparently complete and without material impairment of function.

General arc light irradiation is of the greatest value in these cases because of its richness in ultra-violet rays, the effects of which are especially needed in these cases to promote calcium metabolism. For best effects applications should be sufficiently intense to produce a pronounced erythema of the whole skin surface. This is best accomplished by treating circumscribed areas in succession until the whole surface has been gone over. A good plan is to begin with a third degree erythema covering the affected joint or limb. An application of the same degree of intensity should be made to the abdomen. The next day a similar application may be made to another joint and the back. At the third application the chest and untreated portions of the limbs may be covered and thus within three or four days a pronounced hyperemia of the whole skin surface is produced. The beneficial effects of the strong reactions resulting will generally be noted within a few days. General light applications with gradual increasing intensity may be continued daily or the treatment may be interrupted for a week or ten days until after the erythema induced has for the most part disappeared and then resumed.

For the greatest benefit the application should be made in the open air so that the conditions may approximate as closely as possible to those of the Alpine sun treatment, the enormous value of which in the treatment of disorders of this class has been abundantly demonstrated not only by Rollier but by Rikli, Poncet, Winternitz and others.

Chronic Rheumatism and Osteoarthritis

Under the influence of rest and proper diet and combined with such hydriatic applications as may be indicated in each individual case, phototherapy may accomplish much in this distressing class of ailments. The plan of treatment should include both general and local applications. The general arc light bath and the incandescent cabinet bath may be used on alternate days. Applications to the individual joints may be made with either the arc light or the photophore. In general the application should be intensive. The arc light should be applied in such a way as to produce a third degree erythema. After the surfaces become tanned so that the ultra-violet rays no longer produce a strong reaction, the duration of the arc light application may be lengthened to any extent desired and the intensity of the application may be doubled or quadrupled by cooling the skin surface with a strong air current. The effect of cooling may be intensified by frequently passing a moist cloth over the surface so as to increase evaporation. After the skin surface has become tanned the photophore is almost equally as efficient as the arc light since the chief benefit from light applications is now due to the penetrating luminous and near infra-red rays rather than the ultra-violet. Local applications should be made twice a day or more often if necessary for relief of pain.

When thoroughly applied in connection with other proper remedial measures, light treatment rarely fails to produce beneficial results. Pain, swelling, muscular atrophy and stiffness of joints gradually diminish and often disappear entirely. Even the creaking of joints, which is often a source of much annoyance to patients, often entirely disappears.

The beneficial results obtained from light treatment are less pronounced in cases of rheumatism deformans, or osteoarthritis, than in the simple forms of rheumatism in which the bony structures are involved. However, when the treatment can be continued thoroughly for several months until the skin is strongly pigmented, it may be expected that the progress of the disease will be arrested and in most cases a very considerable degree of improvement secured. Of course it is necessary in every case to make a thorough search for focal infections and to see that such foci are removed.

Special attention must be given to the dietary of the patient. The patient must adhere to a strictly antitoxic diet. The flora must be changed and kept changed so that intestinal putrefactions are suppressed. This is highly important for in the writer's experience chronic colitis exists in the great majority of cases. The ileocecal valve is incompetent so that the infection extends far up in the small intestine and thus the blood is constantly contaminated by bacteria and bacterial products absorbed from the lower ileum. The writer has often seen rheumatic symptoms gradually disappear after the cure of colonic infection by change of the intestinal flora and the systematic use of hot colonic irrigations. Light applications applied in the manner above indicated are far more effective in the treatment of joint affections than hot air applications.

The results of phototherapy in disease of the joints are far superior to the Bier's method. A much more intense degree of local hyperemia can be induced than by the application of the elastic bandage, and without any of the risks or inconveniences of the latter method. There is no danger of overdoing the treatment even if the application is carried to the point of producing so-called erythema or photo-dermatitis. The most intense leucocytosis is produced, and a durable vascular activity which is most conducive to recovery.

The most efficient measures for relieving this distressing condition are rest in bed and intensive applications of heat to the lower back by means of the arc light and the photophore. The arc light should be applied in such a way as to produce a third degree erythema over an area covering the whole middle of the lower part of the back. Intensive applications by means of the photophore and the cooling air current should be applied daily or twice a day. The intensive applications of the arc light may be repeated every five to seven days.

Focal infections must be sought for. Not infrequently a diseased colon will be found to be the real seat of the trouble. A rectal ulcer, a colitis or a diseased appendix may be the real cause of lumbago either through infection or through reflex action.

Intestinal stasis, clearly indicated by infrequent or putrid smelling stoods, must be corrected. The bowels should be made to move three or four times a day by the use of fresh vegetables, fruits, Fig Bran, agar and other laxatives, including paraffin preparations for lubrication. The flora should be changed by the use of lactose or Lacto-Dextrin and an antitoxic diet, excluding meat and eggs.

Muscular Rheumatism

Intensive applications of both the arc light and the incandescent light render invaluable service in the treatment of this condition. Intensive applications are required as in the case of lumbago. The cause must be sought for first of all in some focus of infection such as a diseased tonsil or a diseased tooth. Not infrequently an infected colon, the seat of colitis, is the real mischief maker.

Backache

The pain in the back from which many persons, particularly women, often suffer greatly, which is generally attributed to pelvic disease, is in the writer's opinion more frequently due to chronic disease of the colon or rectum, the result of intestinal stasis. Fecal matters too long retained undergo putrefaction and the result is infection of the intestinal mucous membrane which, in aggravated form, is known as colitis. The same sort of infection, though less intense, is probably present in the majority of cases of chronic constipation. When the irritation becomes so great that the colon becomes spastic this state of spasm is frequently accompanied by a severe pain in the back. Spasm of the intestine produces reflex pain in the lumbar region, sometimes also in the limbs in precisely the same manner that spasm of the pylorus produces pain at the epigastrium.

For relief of this type of pain electric-light applications should be made over the entire abdomen. An erythema of the third degree should be produced and this should be repeated after six or seven days. At the same time the intestinal flora should be changed and an antitoxic diet should be adopted, avoiding meat and eggs, and the colon should be washed out daily by an enema consisting of two quarts of water at a temperature of 115° to 120° F.

Ultra-Violet Rays in Calcium Deficiency—Rickets

The observations of Hess, Steenbock and many others have clearly shown the remarkable influence of ultra-violet rays in stimulating the calcium metabolism. This is a clear indication for the use of the arc light in all cases in which there is deficient assimilation. Young infants suffering from rickets should receive arc light treatment once or twice a week until the symptoms disappear. Great care must be exercised in the application of the arc light to very young infants to avoid injury. The first exposures should be very short, not more than one minute. The time of the exposure may be gradually lengthened as the infant's skin becomes accustomed to contact with the ultra-violet rays.

No doubt nearly all infants born in that portion of the United States known as the Great Lake region will be benefited by the systematic application of the arc light in the manner suggested. It is more than probable that such a use of light would add considerably to the average stature of the population. Pregnant and nursing mothers as well as young infants should receive regularly at least once a week general applications of the arc light. In regions where the annual amount of sunshine is so small as in the Great Lake region and the Northwest, every public school should be provided with the arc light and all young children should be subjected to the protective influence of this powerful vitalizing agent at least once a week during the months of December, January, February, March and April.

Fractures

Light applications, both general and local, have received less consideration in the treatment of fractures than they deserve. After a serious injury of this sort the patient is often necessarily confined to his bed for several weeks, sometimes even several months. The natural effect of this enforced inactivity is a marked deterioration in the patient's general physical condition. Metabolism is slowed, elimination is diminished, the voluntary muscles atrophy from disuse, the heart muscle becomes weakened, the appetite often fails, the bowels become inactive, cathartics are resorted to, colitis is a natural consequence, the bowels become spastic, intense toxemia develops, the patient feels "bilious," often becomes depressed, nervous and a victim of insomnia; and when the fracture is finally united he often finds himself so depleted in general health as to be quite unfit to resume his accustomed activities. The injured limb is often swollen and the seat of pain; the joints are stiffened and surrounded with exudate to such an extent that the tissues are often almost as hard as wood. Not infrequently the fracture fails to unite or makes only a fibrous union because of the failure of calcium metabolism.

General and local applications of light afford the best possible means of combating all these evils. The vitalizing and rejuvenating effect of the general light bath aids greatly in counteracting the effects of inactivity. As numerous observers have pointed out, the ultra-violet rays not only prevent muscular atrophy but may even cause a great increase in the volume and the density of muscular tissues even without exercise.

The light applications should begin within a week after the occurrence of the fracture. It is perhaps wise to permit the process of consolidation to get a start before beginning general applications, but local applications may be made with benefit.

The writer has for many years practiced the application of heat in some form in all cases of fracture before attempting to adjust the bones or applying a permanent dressing. Either the arc light or the photophore affords the most efficient means of applying heat in these cases because of the highly penetrating character of the luminous and infra-red heat rays. Intensive applications are best, the surface being cooled by a continuous air current. Such an application continued for 15 or 20 minutes relieves pain, lessens spasm and so greatly facilitates the reduction of the fracture that with gentle manipulation the bones may be brought perfectly in place without the aid of an anesthetic. General light applications to the trunk and uninjured limbs may be made daily with advantage from the beginning of the patient's confinement in bed, and after 10 or 12 days the permanent dressing may be with care removed long enough to permit an application of light to the injured parts. The application of the arc light should be sufficiently intense to produce a second degree erythema. After the application the parts may be dusted with talcum powder.

The effect of these local light applications will be to encourage the production of callus, to prevent muscular atrophy, to hasten the absorption of exudates which may have resulted from bruising of the tissues, and to lessen pain. By continuing the applications after removal of the dressing, the recovery of the full use of the parts will be greatly facilitated.

Light applications, both general and local, are particularly valuable in cases of ununited fracture and in cases of pseudarthrosis. Phototherapy may also render great service in cases of comminuted compound fractures. In infected cases of compound fracture the arc light should be applied two or three times daily, for two or three minutes at first, the time being gradually increased from day to day. The raw surfaces should be kept clean by daily irrigation with normal saline solution. After the light application the parts should be sprinkled with lactose or Lacto-Dextrin, a mixture of equal parts of lactose and dextrin. The raw surfaces should not be thickly covered with dressing but should be exposed and protected by a wire cage.

Sprains and Dislocations

Local light applications are of the greatest service in the treatment of joints which have been injured by sprain or dislocation. After the injured parts have been replaced, intensive light applications should be made twice daily. Either the arc light or the photophore may be employed. It is a good plan to make at the beginning an arc light application of sufficient intensity to produce third degree erythema and then to follow this up with applications of the incandescent light by the photophore two or three times a day. In the intervals between the light applications the injured parts should be protected with a cotton compress covered by mackintosh or oiled silk, or, better, by the heating compress or so-called water poultice.

Hemophilia

In hemophilia the arc light treatment should be given with the hope of improving the coagulating properties of the blood by increasing the intake of lime.

Sprue

In sprue, another calcium deficiency disease, light treatment should be employed in connection with the use of parathyroid extract and proper regulation of the diet.

Phototherapy in Tuberculosis

The success of the open air and sun treatment of tuberculosis is one of the notable triumphs of modern scientific medicine. Thanks to the work of Finsen, Reyn, Rollier and numerous others, this method of dealing with cases of tubercular infection has become known to the whole civilized world and has been the means of saving many thousands of sufferers who otherwise would have been doomed to an early death.

The results obtained by this mode of treatment have really been so wonderful as to be almost incredible. The accompanying cuts made from photographs kindly given the author by Dr. Rol-

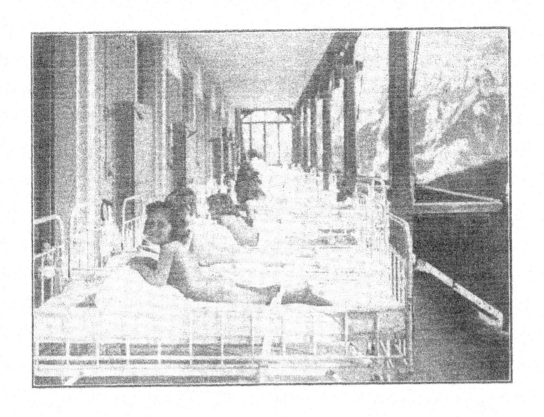

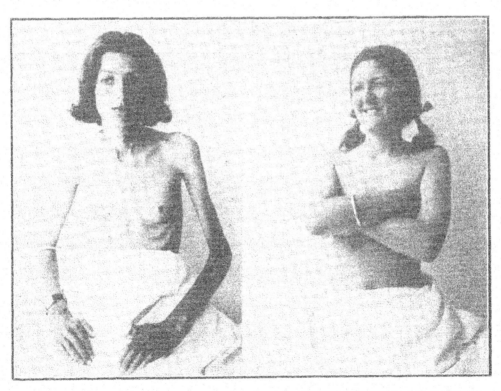

SUN AND OPEN-AIR TREATMENT OF TUBERCULOSIS AT LEYSIN, SWITZERLAND (ROLLIER)

lier, of Leysin, on the occasion of a visit to that world-famous resort, will give a faint impression of the miracles wrought by the simplest of natural agencies—light, air, rest and proper food under the control of skilled medical supervision.

Equally remarkable results have been obtained at the Finsen Institute, of Copenhagen, where special attention has been given to the treatment of lupus, the good results of which are illustrated in several of the accompanying cuts. When the writer first visited the Finsen Institute in 1899, soon after it was opened, the sun was largely depended upon as a source of light, but at the present time, as I found on my last visit (1926), as for many years back, the light of the carbon arc lamp is employed almost altogether. Sunshine is so uncertain and its intensity so variable it is vastly less suited to accurate scientific work than is light from an arc lamp of the most approved pattern, which is absolutely uniform and dependable.

Abundant clinical experience has shown that even in the treatment of tuberculosis the arc light may take the place of the sun. It is to be remembered, however, that in the treatment of tuberculosis as practiced by Rollier, exposure of the skin to the air is an important factor. Often, in cases in which exposures to the direct rays of the sun may be of short duration, not more than 15 minutes perhaps, the skin may be exposed to the air and to the light reflected from the sky for many hours. In the opinion of the writer little can be expected in the treatment of these cases unless the open air treatment is combined with the light therapy. To give general and local applications of the arc light in a case of tubercular disease of a joint while keeping the patient indoors in an overheated atmosphere should not, in the writer's opinion, be expected to result otherwise than in failure. To attain success in dealing with these cases it is necessary that the patient should have the benefit of the air treatment as well as the arc light application. It is highly important that this should be borne in mind for, unfortunately, there are large areas in the United States in which the sky is overcast with clouds so large a proportion of the time that the sun can be depended upon as a source of light for therapeutic applications only during a few weeks of the year, hence, in these regions at least, it is necessary to depend upon the arc light as a source for ultra-violet rays. During the warmer months the arc light may be administered in the open air and thus all the good results obtainable by the open air sun treatment in Alpine regions may be secured.

The remarkable influence of light in increasing the assimilation of lime is doubtless one means by which it produces its remarkable curative effects in tuberculosis. It is known that one of the principal ways in which the body defends itself against tubercle-bacillus is by surrounding it with lime, shutting it off from contact with the tissues. The tubercle bacillus secretes a waxy substance with which it encases itself and so acquires efficient protection against the attacks of the white blood corpuscles which readily destroy most other forms of bacteria. This wax overcoat protects the tubercle bacillus so efficiently that the white cell after swallowing it, is unable to digest it, so that the bacillus may actually grow and thrive in the body of the white cell until it is able to destroy it by the deadly toxins which it produces. For this reason Nature is compelled to supply another means of combating the tubercle bacillus, and lime is necessary for building a barricade to imprison these destructive organisms.

There is no other means known by which the ability of the body to appropriate lime may be so wonderfully aided as by applications of ultra-violet light to the skin. As is well-known, it is by this means that infants suffering from rickets are so quickly completely cured by applications of ultra-violet light. There is considerable ground for believing that an inadequate calcium metabolism may be a predisposing cause of tuberculosis infection and one of the reasons for the inability of the body to successfully combat the infection after it has occurred.

The wonderful effect of light applications in increasing the immunizing properties of the blood is undoubtedly another powerful factor in the beneficial influence of light in cases of tuberculous infection. General applications of light are beneficial in all forms of tuberculous infection and have been shown by clinical experience to be of greater importance than local applications.

However, there are several special photo-therapeutic indications in each particular class of tubercular infection.

The enormous clinical experience at Leysin, Copenhagen, and Berck-Plage, have placed the photo-therapeutic treatment of open tuberculosis upon a thoroughly systematic and scientific foundation.

It is necessary to remember, however, that in the employment of light in the treatment of these cases the well established principles of orthopedic surgery are not to be ignored. The various ingenious mechanical appliances which have been devised by orthopedic surgeons for use in these cases find useful employment. The chief thing which has been eliminated by the development of the light treatment in this class of cases is the multilating surgery which formerly made lifelong cripples in numberless cases, which by light therapy are now restored to complete functional soundness, although ugly scars may remain as relics of the fierce struggle with a destructive adversary which has been waged.

For explicit directions for dealing with this class of cases the reader is referred to the classical work of Rollier, although it must be added that no one can consider himself competent to deal with this most interesting class of cases without an opportunity for extended observation and study at such clinics as Leysin and Berck-Plage.

Pulmonary Tuberculosis

For a long time after the value of light treatment in cases of skin and bone tuberculosis had been clearly established, the impression prevailed that lung tuberculosis was a distinct contra-indication for light treatment. This, however, has been proven to be an error. Says Rollier, "Twenty years of experience have convinced me that patients with pulmonary tuberculosis do not suffer in the least from exposure to sunlight. Not once has there been a mishap of any kind; on the contrary, a striking improvement under the influence of the correctly administered sun bath has been the rule in every case."

The fact that persons suffering from tuberculosis of the bones, joints or skin make excellent recoveries under light treatment and remain well for many years, is in itself a proof of the curative influence of light treatment in cases of lung tuberculosis, for the reason that careful examination of persons suffering from bone or skin tuberculosis shows in nearly every case involvement of the lungs; that is, persons who have bone tuberculosis also have tuberculosis of the lungs, and when recovery from the infection of the bones occurs, recovery from the lung infection takes place at the same time.

In the treatment of his patients Rollier takes care to avoid producing an erythema, while Reyn, on the other hand, considers the production of erythema necessary to secure the most rapid and complete results. Leonard Hill, who spent some months at Leysin and made extensive experimental studies, has demonstrated the immunizing effect of a pronounced erythema. It is probable, however, that benefit is derived from applications of light to the skin no matter how the application is made, provided, however, that so massive a dose is not given as to produce a febrile condition. It is clear that care should be taken to avoid producing a severe general erythema. A non-febrile patient may receive a dose sufficient to produce an erythema of the first or second degree without injury, and Reyn is of the opinion that a perceptible erythema is necessary in all cases in order to make sure of obtaining the best results.

These views agree with the opinion long held by the writer, who noted more than 30 years ago the necessity for producing erythema in order to secure definite and tangible results. The aim should be to produce an intense tanning of the skin as rapidly as possible. Rollier considers tanning of the skin as an indication that the patient is improving and as a basis for a good prognosis.

In febrile cases the light applications should be very short at first, insufficient to produce any reaction. Each day the duration may be increased. Under this treatment the temperature will in most cases gradually subside. When the temperature becomes normal the duration of the length of seances may be rapidly increased to one or two hours if no depressing effects are observed.

The writer's first clinical observations of the sun treatment of tuberculosis were made more than 30 years ago. One of the early cases was that of a young man who had suffered from lung tuberculosis for a couple of years. Examination showed an extensive involvement of the upper lobe of one lung. He had become very weak and suffered from morning chills, profuse night sweats and an evening rise of temperature to 102° F. and sometimes more. The patient was sent to Colorado with a program which included taking daily sun baths. Within a few weeks he was taking sun baths one or two hours long and exposed his skin to the air and skyshine for several hours daily. Within a few months the patient was notably improved and at the end of two years was able to return to his medical studies, graduated as a physician and for 12 or 15 years reported himself in good health, although later, after returning to his home in Germany, suffered a relapse which carried him off. The relapse was probably due to imprudence as the patient was of a highly erratic disposition and was continually experimenting upon himself.

While light therapy is unquestionably a most precious resource in the treatment of tuberculosis, it must not be regarded in any sense as a panacea, and all measures which have been shown by sound clinical experience to be helpful in combating the disease must be given due consideration.

Rollier lays very great stress upon diet and strongly advises his patients to adopt a lacto-vegetarian diet for the reason that it is non-toxic and thus relieves the body of a very grave handicap.

The writer's observation has been that most persons suffering from tuberculosis have been for many years victims of constipation and are highly toxic. The practice which prevails in most sanitaria of feeding these patients large quantities of meat, the writer considers most detrimental. The advantages of an anti-toxic and basic diet are very great. The kidneys are already overworked because of the large amount of tubercle toxin which they are compelled to eliminate. The post-mortem examinations made at the Phipps Institute, of Philadelphia, have shown that in a large proportion of cases the kidneys are seriously damaged.

It would appear, in fact, that in most cases of death from tuberculosis the patient does not die because he has insufficient lung capacity to live but because of the damage done to his body by the toxins to which his tissues have been long exposed.

In view of these facts it is evident that it would be to the patient's advantage to reduce the burden of toxins which his liver must destroy and his kidneys eliminate as much as possible, and there is no way in which so much can be accomplished in this direction as by the suppression of meats, which are usually already in a state of putrefaction when eaten and which leave in the colon a highly putrefactive residue.

On this account it is of the greatest importance in these cases to change the intestinal flora and to suppress intestinal putrefactions by encouraging elimination. The character of the diet should be such as to encourage bowel action and such food accessories as psyllium seed, Fig Bran and paraffin oil preparations should be used in quantities sufficient to secure three or four bowel movements daily. If necessary to secure complete evacuation of the colon, an enema should be given at bedtime. The greatest care should be taken to avoid intestinal stasis and to manage the diet in such a way that the stools will be practically free from odor.

In the treatment of pulmonary cases it is particularly important to avoid overheating the patient. On this account the arc-light bath is always preferable to the incandescent-cabinet bath. Perspiration should be avoided. The skin should be kept cool by giving the treatment in a cool room or directing a current of air upon the surface of the body during the bath. This precaution is important in all cases in which it is desired to obtain a tonic or restorative effect, but is especially important in cases of tuberlosis. It is doubtless for this reason that Rollier avoids exposing his patients to the sun's rays during the middle hours of the day.

Renal Tuberculosis

Unfortunately this disease is usually far advanced before it is discovered and often the bladder, ureter, and in men even the prostate, seminal vesicles, *vas deferens* and epididymis have become infected. Light treatment is clearly indicated in these cases and certainly renders great service, although it must not be relied upon as the one thing needful. Every known helpful measure must be used, both general and local. The general arc light bath raises resistance and aids in developing immunity. A second or third degree erythema should be induced and repeated every second or third week if possible. Lighter daily applications of the arc light should be made and the patient should live in the open air.

When the kidney is hopelessly involved and has ceased to function, early removal is indicated. When both kidneys are diseased, surgery offers no hope. In such cases it is still possible that substantial benefit may be secured by the arc light or sun and open air treatment. I recall several cases in which these measures have caused the disappearance of all symptoms in cases of well advanced renal tuberculosis and apparent restoration of the patient to sound health.

Of course the closest attention to diet and regimen is necessary in these cases. The flora must be changed and the colon kept free from putrefying residues. This may be easily accomplished by the use of Lacto-Dextrin, Psylla, Fig Bran, and the antitoxic regimen which excludes meat and eggs. It is also wise to reduce the use of cereals to a minimum as Bunge, Blatherwick, Sansum and others have shown that a cereal diet tends to lower the alkali reserve of the body and to increase the acidity of the urine, which is highly unfavorable for the kidneys, especially when they are damaged by disease. A lacto-vegetarian diet should be strictly followed.

Light Treatment in Peritoneal Tuberculosis

These cases, once regarded as hopeless, are now known to be highly amenable to light therapy combined with the open air cure Rest in bed, proper feeding—a lacto-vegetarian dietary—and general arc light applications are measures the persevering employment of which may be looked upon as almost a certain cure for peritoneal and other forms of abdominal tuberculosis. The application should be begun carefully to avoid depressing the patient, but an effort should be made to secure at least a second degree erythema, if not of the whole body at one seance, of the whole skin surface treated in sections, the whole area being gone over within a week. The treatment should be continued until the skin is deeply tanned. The patient should be kept in the open air every moment possible day and night. The flora should be changed and the colon kept thoroughly cleared by the daily use of the enema.

Within a few days of this writing (1927) the author received a call from a handsome, robust young woman who one year ago was in such a condition that she was not expected to live more than a week or two at the most. When first seen she was emaciated almost to the last degree. The abdomen was enormously distended with fluid. The pressure was so great tapping was necessary. The fluid quickly returned and although the case was most unpromising operation was finally decided upon. The surgeon who performed the operation reported that on opening the abdomen he found enormous masses of fibrin and the entire contents of the abdomen covered with tubercles and so firmly matted together that it was impossible to do anything more than to remove as much debris as possible and close the wound. Drainage was left in. The patient's condition was so low that no one expected her to recover from the operation, but with the thought of doing all that could be done arc-light applications were begun at once. A little later sun baths and open-air treatment were given, and three months later the patient had improved to such an extent that she was able to be removed to her home where the sun and open air treatment were continued. The patient adhered strictly to an antitoxic dietary and has gradually improved until at the present time she considers herself in sound health and is able to engage in ordinary household activities. Other similar cases might be mentioned and numerous cases have been reported by other physicians.

There can be no doubt that light therapy is capable of saving a large proportion of these cases, formerly considered the most unpromising of all forms of tuberculous disease.

The Treatment of Tuberculous Lymph Glands

The treatment of tuberculous glands usually found in the neck by removal, while frequently practiced, sometimes with success, has always been open to the objection that disfiguring scars were left and relapses were very frequent. Rollier has demonstrated that light treatment alone is capable of not only arresting the tuberculous process but of causing the disappearance of these glands without surgical interference. When the gland is softened, as not infrequently occurs, the contents may be withdrawn by aspiration and without establishing open drainage. Sometimes the aspiration must be repeated two or three times, but this is a matter of little consequence since no scar is left behind. Even very large glands frequently soften and disappear completely. Sometimes complete absorption occurs so that aspiration is unnecessary. When sinuses have been formed the gland not infrequently becomes saturated and is cast off through the sinus like a foreign body. After this is accomplished the wound gradually closes. Not only superficial glands of the neck are made to disappear by light treatment but those that are deeply seated in the chest also disappear, as shown by X-ray examinations.

The treatment in these cases consists of general applications of light by means of the sun bath or the arc light together with the open air cure, the value of which seems to be in tuberculous cases nearly or quite as important as the light treatment itself.

The Light Treatment of Wounds

The treatment of wounds by protection from the air and abundant dressings is a practice so fortified by long usage and classical teaching that exposure of a wound to the air and light may at first seem to the careful nurse or surgeon as a hazardous proceeding. Of course wounds must be protected from dirt, dust, insects and irritating contacts, but there is no evidence whatever that exposure to the pure air is in the slightest degree detrimental to the healing of a wound.

The effect of light upon an injured surface is highly beneficial, first, because of its stimulating effect upon cell activity. The healing of a wound depends upon cell proliferation. All forms of cell activity respond quickly to the stimulating applications of radiant energy in the form of both light and heat. The reactions induced by the ultra-violet rays, as has been shown by numerous observers, encourage immunization, leukocytosis and the various processes by which the tissues repair their damages and resist the influence of invading bacteria.

In the case of infected wounds the ultra-violet rays have a highly beneficial disinfectant effect. When the rays from an arc light are applied to a suppurating wound, the first effect is to increase the flow of pus. After two or three days the discharge becomes more serous, the pus cells gradually diminish and in a few days the discharge consists of serum only, the surface of the wound becomes covered with a thin protective film and the process of healing proceeds rapidly.

Very indolent wounds require vigorous treatment. The arc light should be applied in such a way as to produce a decided erythema. This will produce at first a very marked increase in suppuration. There will often be noticed a change in the character of the discharge, which will rapidly become lighter in color and soon will lose its offensive odor and within a few days will gradually become thinner until it becomes wholly serous and will then gradually cease altogether.

Inflamed wounds should receive light applications sufficient to produce only first degree erythema. Short applications of light may be made daily, but the more vigorous applications should be made at intervals sufficiently long to permit the reaction produced by one application to nearly disappear before another is made.

The wound should be washed daily with a saturate solution of lactose or Lacto-Dextrin in normal saline solution. When there are sinuses they should be thoroughly washed out with the solution.

Varicose Ulcers

Chronic varicose ulcers of the leg which have long resisted the use of salves, liniments, strappings and various other modes of treatment, even operations, usually heal rapidly under the systematic application of the arc light combined with rest. The patient should remain in a horizontal position and the foot should be elevated 10 or 12 inches to aid the return flow of blood. Both general and local applications of the arc light should be made. The duration of the general applications should be such as to produce a second degree erythema.

Chronic indolent ulcers should receive local applications of sufficient intensity to produce a well pronounced erythema. The general applications may be repeated daily. The more intense local applications should be made about one week apart. During the interval the legs should be exposed to the air, protected by a wire cage.

In cases in which the ulcer is inflamed the local application should be less intense. When there is an abundant purulent discharge this will gradually become more serous until the pus wholly disappears. The serous discharge will gradually diminish, healthy granulations will appear and in most cases healing will be complete at the end of three to six weeks. In some cases the healing process may be greatly promoted by sprinkling lactose or Lacto-Dextrin over the surface or applying a thin compress of cheese-cloth wet with a saturate solution of lactose in normal saline solution.

Syphilitic ulcers usually respond readily to applications of light made in the same manner as directed for varicose ulcers. Of course appropriate specific treatment must be applied at the same time.

It is to be kept in mind that antisyphilitic treatment such as the injection of salvarsan and similar remedies is by no means harmless. The introduction of large quantities of mineral drugs into the circulation does serious damage to the liver and kidneys. This has been clearly demonstrated by efficiency tests. On this account whenever antisyphilitic medication is instituted, sun baths, light baths and other physiologic measures calculated to build up the patient's general health should be simultaneously employed.

The Light Treatment of Burns

It is an interesting fact that burns, even sunburns, are benefited by daily applications of the arc light. The first exposures should be brief, not more than two or three minutes and should be given twice a day. Both general and local applications should be made. The general applications should be such as will produce a first degree erythema. It is well in beginning the treatment to cover the burn with one thickness of cheesecloth. After the first application the cheesecloth need not be employed. The injured surfaces should not be covered with a bandage but should be left exposed to the air, protected, if necessary, by a wire screen.

The Light Treatment of Skin Disorders

Phototherapy has within the last few years come to play almost a dominating role in the treatment of skin affections of almost every sort. The arc light is most efficient. As in most other maladies, the application should be both general and local. For the highest degree of success it is of course necessary that the practitioner should possess a good knowledge of dermatology so that embarrassing mistakes in diagnosis may be avoided.

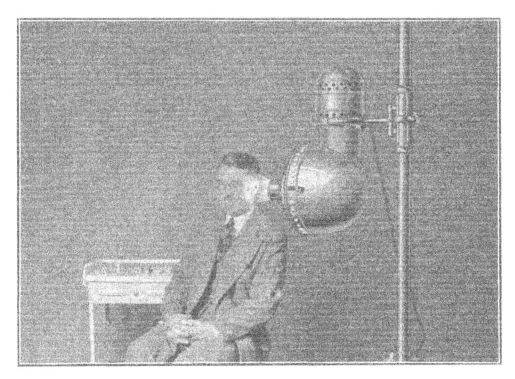

APPLICATION OF ARC LIGHT TO EAR

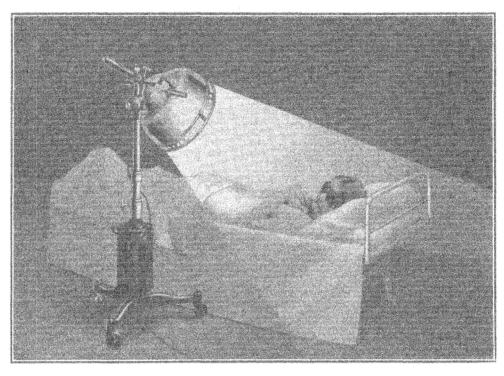

ARC LIGHT TO THE ABDOMEN

Lupus

In the treatment of this disease both general and local applications are necessary. Of the two, general light applications appear to be the most important, but intensive light applications applied directly to the diseased area are also beneficial, at least in certain forms of the disease. The cases which appear to be most benefited by the ultra-violet rays are those belonging to the dry type in which yellowish nodules appear. In the ulcerative type of lupus and in so-called scrofuloderma, X-rays are of the greatest service, but the X-ray should not be employed in the dry type. It is believed that the use of the X-rays in the dry form of lupus may lead to the development of cancer.

In cases of lupus as in other forms of tubercular infection it is of the highest importance that the patient should live in the open air. The sun and open air cure as practiced by Rollier should be employed whenever available. The success of treatment when general light applications and the open air treatment are employed in addition to local measures is 50 per cent greater than when local treatment alone is used.

Psoriasis

This disease, which has resisted so obstinately nearly all other measures of treatment, often yields with the greatest readiness to suitable applications of the arc light. The application should be made with sufficient intensity to produce decided erythema of the skin. The colors will then be reversed—the eruption appearing in the form of white spots on a red ground. In a week or ten days the eruption generally disappears, but it will probably return again unless measures are taken to remove the original causes of the disease, which are generally to be found in an infected condition of the alimentary canal. Care should be taken to regulate the diet so as to cause the disappearance of the putrid odor of the stools. The tongue if coated must become clean, and other symptoms of intestinal autointoxication must be made to disappear. For this a careful antitoxic dietary with the exclusion of flesh foods is essential. The intestinal flora should be changed by the use of Lacto-Dextrin and the bowels should be made to move freely three or four times daily by the use of psyllium seed, Fig Bran and paraffin preparations. When the colon is badly crippled an enema should be administered every night in order to insure complete clearance of residues and wastes.

Before beginning the treatment the patient should have a thorough shampoo and the affected areas should be thoroughly cleared of scales. Great care should be taken to remove all traces of ointments or creams which may have been applied.

Acne Vulgaris

Brilliant results are practically always obtainable in the treatment of acne vulgaris. General light baths of sufficient intensity to produce a second degree erythema with slight peeling of the skin should be given at the beginning of a course of treatment and as the treatment is repeated from day to day the duration of the exposure should be increased. If the first bath is followed by a fairly strong reaction, three or four days may be allowed to elapse to permit the erythema to subside before beginning daily general applications. The local application to the affected skin area should be sufficiently intense to produce an erythema of the third degree. When the skin peels off a considerable degree of improvement will be observed. After a week or two the application may be repeated. A stronger dose will of course be required. After each peeling the number of pimples will be found lessened and in time the last one will disappear.

Pimples that contain pus should be touched with a splinter of wood which has been dipped in pure carbolic acid.

In certain very obstinate cases the light applications may be supplemented by a careful X-ray application by a well informed expert.

In connection with light treatment in these cases general tonic hydriatic treatment should be employed. The patient should be encouraged to exercise much in the open air. The intestinal flora should be changed and an antitoxic diet excluding meat, eggs and much animal fat should be carefully followed. The bowels should be encouraged to move three or four times a day by the free use of Fig Bran, Lacto-Dextrin, psyllium seed and paraffin preparations.

Acne rosacea may sometimes be benefited by light applications, but these cases require most careful handling and should be referred to a skilled dermatologist.

Alopecia—Baldness

While occasional cases have been reported in which baldness of the type which usually begins at the forehead and gradually extends backward, have been successfully treated by ultra-violet light, these cases are exceedingly rare. In general, baldness of this type does not yield satisfactory results to light treatment.

The opposite is true, however, of the form of baldness known as alopecia areata, or patchy baldness. The treatment is very simple. After thorough cleansing of the scalp, first with soap and water, then with pure water so that all grease is removed, the arc light is applied in such a manner as to produce a second or third degree erythema. Each patch of baldness should be treated individually. When there are several patches all may be treated at once or the different areas may be treated in succession, as is most convenient.

Carbuncles—Furunculosis—Boils

Applications of the arc light are indicated in all cases of this sort. In general it is well to begin the treatment with a judicious X-ray application. A single application will often arrest the development of the carbuncle. The arc light should be applied in such a way as to produce an erythema dose of the second or third degree. General light applications should also be employed. In every case the urine should be tested for sugar. If sugar is found present insulin should be administered at once.

Herpes Zoster

The arc light should be applied to the affected area in such a manner as to produce a second or third degree erythema. After the third or fourth day a second application should be made. The pain will usually be lessened by the first application and by repeated applications may be made to disappear entirely.

Light treatment succeeds equally well in the treatment of herpes labialis, herpes preputialis and other forms of herpes.

Lichen Planus

When the papules are prominent, third degree erythema should be produced. Any irritation present may be relieved by repeatedly touching the parts with compresses wrung out of boiling water. In some cases X-ray applications are required. The acute form of the disease usually disappears quickly under mild applications of the arc light such as will produce a first or second degree erythema. The treatment may be applied daily or every other day.

Pityriasis

When the scurfiness is due to infection recovery quickly follows applications of the arc light of sufficient intensity to produce a light erythema. The intensity of the application should be sufficient to produce peeling of the skin. Two or three repetitions of the application will usually be sufficient to effect a cure.

When the cause is dryness of the skin with degeneration of the oil glands, often associated with thyroid deficiency, the ultra-violet light is of little or no value. Cases of this sort may be recognized by the fact that the skin in general is dry because of inactivity of the sweat glands and degeneration of the oil glands. The hair is also dry and brittle.

Urticaria

Urticaria is in the great majority of cases due to sensitization. A careful examination should be made to discover the particular substance or substances to which the patient is sensitized. This must be suppressed. General applications of the arc light or incandescent-cabinet bath may be employed with advantage in connection with other treatment. Immediate relief from the intense itching may be obtained by the application of very hot water or an intensive application of light with the arc light or the photophore.

Itching—Paresthesias

Light is almost a panacea for the distressing itching which accompanies many forms of skin disease, acute and chronic, without or with eruption, and for most of the various paresthesias which accompany certain nervous disorders. The beneficial effect appears to be due to the heat rays, and probably the longer rather than the short rays; that is, the red and inner infra-red.

To be effective, the application must be intensive; that is, the heat must be so great that it can be endured for not more than 3 to 5 seconds or even less. The photophore is the best appliance for use in these cases. A five minute intermittent application is sufficient, in most cases, to relieve the most intense itching, and the relief will last, in most cases, for several hours. It must be remembered that the intensity of the application must be great, sufficient to be slightly painful and to cause a sharp tingling or momentary smarting which will stop the itching at once. The effect of this treatment is not only palliative, but usually develops remarkable curative effects as well. After the treatment lanolin cream or some other suitable protective or emollient remedy should be applied.

Impetigo

The technic is essentially the same as in the treatment of herpes zoster. Care must be taken to remove all crusts and scabs as these will intercept the ultra-violet rays.

Leucoderma-Vitiligo

In this disease there is a loss of pigment in the skin the cause of which is generally supposed to be a toxin of some sort. Combe believed the condition to be due to intestinal toxemia. Other observers have noted that the condition usually makes its appearance after an acute illness, often of a somewhat illy defined character.

The white spots, characteristic of the disease, have convex borders. They usually begin as small white points which slowly increase in size, but sometimes the patches develop rapidly, occasionally reaching the size of a silver dollar or larger, within a few hours.

It is generally stated by skin specialists that leucoderma is most likely to occur on parts exposed to light, such as the face and hands. Hazen advances the theory that the white spots are caused by a ferment which acts as a lysin, dissolving the pigment after having been activated by the sunlight. The observation of Hill and Eidinow that erythema doses of light notably increase the immunizing power of the blood and tissue fluids led me to think that such doses of light might render service in these cases. I have since had opportunity to treat two cases, one a man of thirty-five, by sunlight, the other, a lady of fifty, by the arc light. In the case of the man the white spots appeared upon the thighs and feet, parts not exposed to light. Within two weeks after beginning daily sun baths, the large white patches on his thighs showed many small brown spots about the size of a pin head. Three weeks later the spots had enlarged until they began to run together as shown in the accompanying illustration. The improvement continued until the spots were nearly obliterated.

In the case of the lady the spots appeared upon the hands, forearms and front of the chest and abdomen. Marked improvement began after the application of the arc light for about five weeks. When last seen the spots had nearly disappeared, being gradually obliterated by the running together of the small spots which appeared scattered over the whole depigmented area and grew rapidly until the color of the skin was nearly restored to normal.

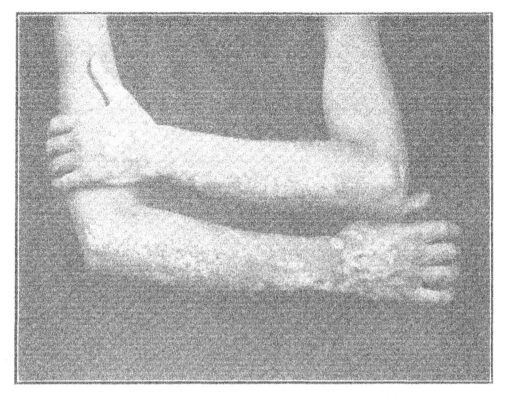

CASE OF LEUCODERMA TREATED BY ARC LIGHT. MARKED IMPROVEMENT
SEEN IN ARMS

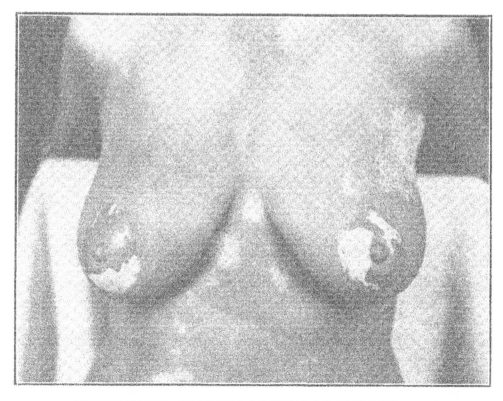

LEUCODERMIA SHOWING RETURN OF PIGMENT UNDER
LIGHT TREATMENT

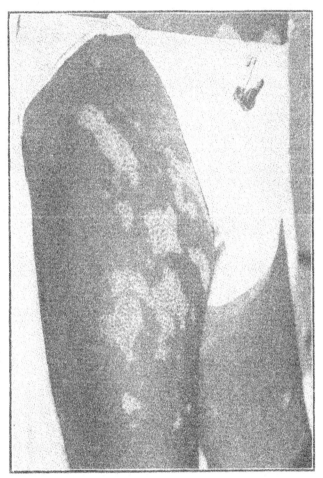

THE SAME CASE THREE WEEKS LATER

The after history of these cases is not known, but the results observed certainly justify the hope that moderately severe doses of light may prove beneficial in these cases which have heretofore been regarded as incurable. Says Hazen: "No form of treatment, either external or internal has the slightest effect." The same author adds, "the patient should not expose himself to sunlight," the very thing he ought to do. It must be remembered, also, that the application must be an erythema dose in order to produce any tangible effect.

It should be added that in addition to light treatment in these cases the flora must be changed and an antitoxic regimen faithfully followed. This is easily accomplished by the elimination of meat and eggs from the bill of fare, and the adoption of efficient means to increase the activity of the colon. Psyllium seed, bran and mineral oil in some form are the most efficient of laxative food accessories and may be used indefinitely without injury. To these measures must be added the use of lactose or lacto-dextrin to encourage the rapid development of a protective acidophile flora in the intestine.

I have seen marked improvement in a number of cases of vitiligo when these measures alone were used, no light applications being made, a fact which appears to confirm the theory that the disease may be of intestinal origin. The colon is a veritable incubator of virulent poisons which may play a much larger rôle in the etiology of disease than many physicians are at present willing to admit.

Chloasma—Liver Spots

This condition is the opposite of the preceding; viz., an increase of pigment in circumscribed areas of the skin. It may be distinguished from leucoderma by the fact that the borders of the affected areas are concave instead of convex.

Such causes as syphilis, tuberculosis and ovarian disease must be removed. The chloasma of pregnancy soon disappears after the pregnancy terminates. Any unbalance of the internal secretions must be corrected. To these measures may be added with good results the same treatment recommended for leucoderma. The first light application should be of sufficient intensity to cause a pronounced erythema and free peeling of the epidermis. Special attention must be given to diet and changing the intestinal flora. With thorough and persevering treatment good results may be expected.

Sycosis

Light therapy is employed in the treatment of this disease in connection with the X-ray. After a proper X-ray dose has been applied applications of sufficient intensity to produce a second degree erythema may be made at intervals of three to five days.

Onychia

An erythema dose of the third degree is required. The application should be repeated after five to seven days or as soon as the reaction produced has subsided.

Pruritus Ani—Pruritus Vulvae

The parts should be thoroughly cleansed with soap and water night and morning and after each bowel movement. After such cleansing an arc light dose sufficient to produce a third degree erythema should be applied. At the end of a week a second similar dose should be applied and the treatment should be repeated twice weekly, the time of the application being increased at each seance. For temporary relief very hot water should be applied in the manner described elsewhere. (See Index.)

Chilblains

Light applications are highly valuable in cases of this sort both curatively and as a prophylactic measure. The application should be of such intensity as to produce a second degree erythema. The treatment should be repeated after five or six days. When the skin is broken, paraffin wax dressing should be applied for protection.

The purpose of the treatment is to stimulate the blood circulation. The alternate hot and cold foot bath may be advantageously employed in connection with the light treatment. This powerful revulsive measure rapidly improves the vascular tone, which is always deficient in this condition.

Bright's Disease

In Bright's disease and cardiovascular-renal disease light applications may render service but must be employed with very great care. It is particularly important to avoid overheating the patient on account of the depressing influence of heat upon the heart. General light applications of the arc light or the incandescent-light cabinet may be employed two or three times a week advantageously as a means of producing tonic effects. The intensity of the arc light should be only sufficient to produce a reaction of the first degree. The duration of the incandescent-cabinet bath should be sufficient only to heat the skin, perhaps barely starting perspiration, but without causing a rise of the body temperature. A light erythema, second degree, may be produced over the back and the upper abdomen. The area involved should not be more than one square foot. Great care should be taken to avoid prolonging the application sufficiently to produce a depressing effect.

In the treatment of this disease it is to be remembered that in many cases, the cause is to be found in overwork of the kidneys in their effort to keep the blood free from toxins which have been introduced in excessive quantities, or have been generated within the body. The most common source of these toxic substances is the intestinal canal, where they are the result of the putrefaction of food residues.

The use of flesh foods, even of eggs in excessive quantities, may be a cause of these putrefactions; hence in the treatment of this disease, reliance should not be placed upon light treatment alone or any other measure which deals only with the symptoms or the results of the malady, but an effort should be made to remove the cause.

The diet should be thoroughly antitoxic; meat should be wholly excluded, also coffee, tea and alcohol in all forms.

The use of alcohol and tobacco are without doubt potent etiological factors in many cases of renal disease. It is to be remembered, also, that in many cases, perhaps the majority, the primary cause of premature failure of the kidney is damage due to an attack of scarlet fever, measles or some other infectious disease occurring in childhood.

Whatever may be the cause of the disease, it is evident that in its treatment a matter of the very first importance is to lighten so far as possible the burden of these generally overworked organs.

In these cases it is of the highest importance that the intestinal flora should be changed. An antitoxic diet, discarding meat and eggs, should be permanently adopted. In some cases it is decidedly advantageous, as has been shown by Sansum, to adopt a strictly basic diet which requires not only the exclusion of meat and eggs but the greatly restricted use of cereals. By this means the alkali reserve of the blood is increased and the labor of the kidneys in the removal of acid residues is greatly diminished.

Light Treatment in Arteriosclerosis and High Blood Pressure

Light applications to the general surface of the body either by the arc light or the incandescent light are of far greater value in arteriosclerosis than any other external measure which can be applied. The effect of the application is to dilate the surface vessels, thus relieving the heart, while at the same time all the functional activities of the body are quickened and thus the cause of the disease is combated. The most thoroughgoing effects are produced by the application of the arc light to successive areas of the skin, going over the whole surface of the body in the course of a week. The intensity of the application should be sufficient to produce a moderate degree of erythema. This permanent dilatation of the vessels greatly relieves the work of the heart in cases of hypertension. The application is of equal value in cases of secondary low pressure, although in these cases the beneficial results will be manifested not in lowering the pressure, but in increasing cardiac efficiency by lessening the amount of work required of the heart. Not infrequently the improvement is later shown in a preliminary rise of blood pressure, showing the increase of cardiac energy; but if the treatment is continued, a subsequent fall in blood pressure occurs as a result of the opening of the blood vessels and the oxidation and elimination of the toxins to which the diseased state of the vessels is due. The fall in blood pressure sometimes occurs within a short time after the beginning of the treatment, doubtless due to the lessening of the toxic products in circulation through the vessels, the presence of which gives rise to spasm of the small vessels through irritation of the vasomotor centers.

In the treatment of cases of arteriosclerosis and high blood pressure it is well to remember that Sansum and others have demonstrated that a marked lowering of the blood pressure may be secured by the adoption of a basic dietary. This excludes meats and eggs and to a large extent cereals from the bill of fare because these foods leave an acid residue in the body and thus reduce the alkali reserve and greatly increase the amount of work required of the kidneys in the elimination of acid residues. The writer has made use of a basic diet in the treatment of cases of this sort for more than 40 years and has seen most excellent results in hundreds of cases.

Raynaud's Disease

The beneficial effects of light treatment in cases of this sort are frequently almost magical. The writer recalls a case of this disease treated years ago (1902), a young woman, a school teacher about 20 years of age. The toes of both feet were affected, those of the left foot more severely than the right. The little toe of the left foot had been amputated, one joint of the fourth toe had been lost, the third toe was black and cold and the remaining toes were evidently very poorly supplied with blood. The light from a carbon arc lamp was applied to the toes of both feet three times a week, care being taken to avoid more than a very slight reaction. Circulation in the feet improved at once. Within a few days the dark color began to disappear from the toes, which assumed a pinkish hue, and within a month the tissues were normal in appearance, the feet were warm and a cure seemed assured. I saw and examined this patient more than 15 years later and was glad to learn that there had been no return of the disease.

Diseases of Women

In most of the chronic ailments to which women are especially subject, the general arc-light bath may be employed with great advantage. A large share of these ailments are the result of a general lowering of vital resistance, impaired nutrition, an anemic state of the blood, slowed metabolism, inadequate elimination and other conditions which are most efficiently combated by phototherapy.

Ailments which are due to infection, parturient injuries or the development of neoplasms, present special indications which must be met by surgical or other means, but even in these cases light applications may render great assistance in increasing the patient's vital resistance and promoting remedial processes.

Many years of clinical experience have taught the writer that in the great majority of cases the distresses of which women complain are due to colitis, toxemia, or other causes rather than to the pelvic organs to which they attribute their discomforts.

Dysmenorrhea

The menstrual pain from which many young women and married women who have not borne children suffer usually disappears after the skin has been well tanned by exposure to the sun or to the ultra-violet rays of the general arc-light bath. For immediate relief the arc light or the photophore applied intensively to the lower abdomen or the back often affords quick relief. A still more effective measure is an application of radiant heat to the hips and legs. The intensity of the application should be as great as can be borne without discomfort, as the higher the temperature the more positive the inhibitory effects produced.

Amenorrhea

In this condition there is usually a disturbance of the endocrine functions. The powerful influence of general light applications upon the function of the endocrine glands has been clearly shown, especially in relation to the glands associated with reproduction. Steenbock and others have shown that the egg production of chickens may be doubled by exposure to the ultra-violet rays. Milk production in cattle has been increased. Arctic travelers have noted that the Eskimo women cease to menstruate during the long winter night. The general arc-light bath should be administered in such a way as to produce a second degree erythema. Within three or four days the dose should be repeated with increased intensity. The bath may be given daily until the skin is well pigmented. It is also well to make local applications over the lower abdomen once or twice a week with sufficient intensity to produce a third degree erythema. Similar applications may be made to the back likewise.

The beneficial effects of the light treatment may be greatly intensified by the application of a cold douche to the hips and legs. The temperature should be 50° to 60° F. and the duration of the application 5 to 10 seconds. The feet and legs should be warm when the cold application is made. After the application the patient should be dried quickly and the limbs should be thoroughly rubbed to insure a good reaction.

The restoration of the menstrual function may be greatly hastened in these cases by the use of diathermy. One electrode should be placed upon the lower back and the other internally.

Diet in Connection With Light Treatment

The importance of regulating the diet in connection with therapeutic applications of light cannot be overestimated. The writer is pleased to find that an authority so thoroughly scientific and resourceful as Doctor Rollier has reached essentially the same conclusion as himself in relation to the dietary which should be employed in connection with light.

Says Rollier in the latest edition of his most excellent work, "Heliotherapy": "In the practice of heliotherapy, therefore, rules of diet must be laid down. The patient must be persuaded to reduce the amount of food taken and, above all, restrict his consumption of meat. Heavy viands, game, etc., are strictly banned from our bill of fare. Our patients receive white meat, preferably cold. In summer the diet is planned mostly on vegetarian lines. Cereals (bread, oats, barley, etc.), being extremely nourishing, without being toxic, should form the basis of a rational diet throughout the treatment just as they do in the diet of races inhabiting hot climates. They are well tolerated by patients of all ages and even by the weakest stomachs. Vegetables must never be omitted, because they supply the organism with necessary and easily assimilable phosphates and other salts. Green foods are known to mitigate constipation and to contribute to the maintenance of the calcium content, besides supplying in an inexpensive form the body's demand for magnesium, potassium and iron. Fruit is considered by us to be an absolutely indispensable item of the patient's diet. We see to it that fruit is served at breakfast as well as at supper. If eaten the first thing in the morning, its slightly aperient effect is highly beneficial. It is also most refreshing when eaten during the sun bath. Alcohol and tobacco are not compatible with heliotherapy and are, therefore, forbidden."

When visiting Leysin recently (1926), I was informed by Rollier's chief assistant that he advises his patients to discard the use of meats entirely, although he does not absolutely insist that they must do so but is highly pleased when they do.

Intensive Phototherapy

When I discovered in 1891 the superior value of the electric light as a source of heat I soon observed that overheating of the skin surface was a serious obstacle in the way of securing the highest degree of efficiency for the reason that it prevented the use of a sufficient volume of heat to influence strongly the deeper tissues. I endeavored to overcome the difficulty in various ways

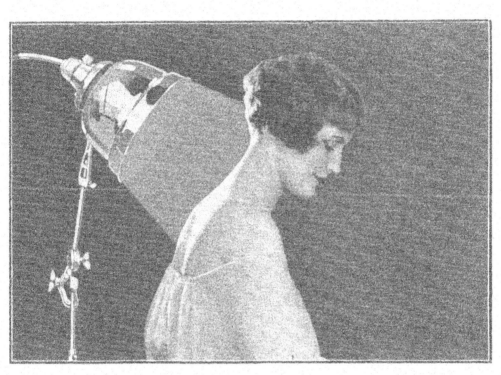

APPLICATION OF PHOTOPHORE TO UPPER SPINE

and finally solved the problem by directing upon the treated surface a current of air.

Many years ago Conrad Klar showed by experiments with the calorimeter that when the body is exposed to an atmosphere the temperature of which is below that of the body, the rate of heat elimination during the first five minutes is increased to more than ten times the normal. After the first five minutes the rate of heat elimination is reduced to about five times the normal through the contraction of the surface vessels, whereby the amount of blood circulating through the skin is diminished. These observations show clearly the high degree of efficiency of an air current in cooling the skin.

By this means I was able to double and even quadruple the volume of heat radiation employed in treatment. This means that by simple cooling of the skin quantities of heat may be applied which would otherwise be absolutely intolerable and would give rise to destruction of tissue if long continued, and without the slightest injury to the skin tissues or any interference with the passage of the penetrating heat rays to the deeper structures.

From the above it must be evident that the combination of the cooling air current with applications of radiant energy from the arc light or the incandescent lamp or photophore is a matter of very great practical importance. This statement is clearly borne out by clinical experience. In cases in which no relief from pain is obtainable by ordinary hot applications, the massive doses of radiant energy which may be employed by this method cause it quickly to disappear. This intensive method of applying heat is especially valuable in cases of deep seated pain as in chronic sciatica and in certain cases of visceral disease.

This method was first used by the writer about 25 years ago (1902) and was described in an earlier edition of this work published in 1910. It was also described in a more recent paper presented at the last annual meeting of the American Electrotherapeutic Association (1927).

Index

Abdominal viscera, effect of heat
   on 77
Acne vulgaris 191
Air bath 148
Air douche 147
Aknaton 9
Alopecia 195
Amenorrhea 204
Anemia 158
Arc cabinet bath............. 106
Arc light 27, 96, 103
  applications 106
Arteriosclerosis 202

Backache 176
Bacteria, effects of light on.... 28
Baldness 195
Boils 195
Blood, effect of heat on....... 75
  effect of light on........... 48
Blood pressure, high.......... 202
Blood vessels, effect of light on 47
Bones, disease of............. 172
Bright's disease 201
Bronchitis 169
Burns, light treatment of...... 192

Cachexias 153
Calcium deficiency 177
Carbuncles 195
Chemical rays 28
Chilblains 200
Chloasma 199
Chorea 171
Chlorosis 158
Colitis 162
Cold douche 139
Colored light 33

Diabetes 155
Dislocations 190
Dismenorrhea 204
Douche, cold 139

Effects of light on eye........ 42
Electric light bath............ 55
  invention of 60
Epilepsy 166

Erythema, solar 34
  therapeutic use of.......... 114
Exophthalmic goiter 159

Fever, convalescence 151
Fluorescence 20
Fractures 178
Furunculosis 195

Gall-bladder disease 160
Goiter, exophthalmic 159

Half sheet rub................ 147
Heat, effects on blood......... 75
  effects on circulation 74
  effects on muscles 73
  effects on nervous system 73
  effects on respiration 76
  effects on the skin 72
  effects on temperature 76
  inhibits pain 81
  intermittent 130
  with fan 129
Heat rays, luminous........... 16
  non-luminous 16
  penetrating effects ......61 to 67
Hemoglobin, light effect on.... 49
Hemophilia 180
Herpes zoster 196
Hyperacidity 159
Hysteria 166

Incandescent bath 116, 127
Indigestion 161, 162
Infra-red rays 22, 53, 62, 119
  effects on bacteria 30
Insomnia 172
Impetigo 197
Iridescence 19
Itching 197

Joints, disease of............. 172

Kidneys, effect of heat on...... 79
  tuberculosis of............. 187

Leukoderma 198
Leucocytosis 48
Lichen planus 196
Light, applications of.......... 89

209

bath in bed 126
bath, incandescent 116
  colored 25
  cosmetic effect of........... 42
  effects on animal life........ 31
  effects on plants............ 24
  effect on skin glands........ 45
  infra-red 12
  effects influenced by heat..... 44
  physics of 11
  physiologic effects 23
  rays, classification 13
  sources of 14
  therapy 68
  therapeutic use discovered.... 10
Liver, cirrhosis of........... 162
  effect of heat on........... 79
Locomotor ataxia 166
Luminescence 20
Luminous heat rays........... 66
Lung tuberculosis 183
Lupus 193
Lymph glands, tuberculous 189

Melancholia 170
Mercury arc 131
Metabolism, effect of heat on.. 80
  effect of light on............ 46
Mitten friction 143
Migraine 168
Muscles, effect of heat on..... 73
Myelitis 165
Myxedema 172

Nerves, effect of light on...... 51
Neuralgia 165
Neurasthenia 167
Neuritis 164

Obesity 156
Onychia 200
Osteo-arthritis 174

Pain, gastric 161
  inhibited by heat 81
  intensive application for..... 128
Paresthesias 197
Peptic ulcer 160
Phosphorescence 20
Photo erythema 114
Photophore 124
Phototherapy, clinical 151
Phototherapy, intensive 206
Pigmentation, benefits of....... 39
Pityriasis 196
Pleurisy 170
Pruritis ani 200
Pruritis vulva 200

Psoriasis 193
Psychosis 200

Quartz light 131

Radiant heat, discovery of the
  use of 53
Radiantor 127
Reproduction, effect of light on 52
Reynaud's disease 203
Rheumatism 174
Rheumatism, muscular 176
Rickets 177

Salt glow 142
Sand bath 94
Shallow bath 141
Skin, changes in............. 41
  cooling of 100
  organ of defense 43
  pigmentation of 37
  reflex areas of 87
  reflex relations 83
  sensitization 40
  treatment of 192
Sonne 62
Spectrum 11
Sprue 180
Strains 180
Sun bath 89
Sunlight 16
  intensity of 18

Temperature, color scale....... 15
Thermic rays, physiologic effects
  of 70
Thermotherapy 69, 135
Towel rub 144
Tuberculosis 180
  abdominal 188
  lung 183
  renal 187

Ulcer, varicose 191
Ultra-violet light 16, 20
  sources of 17
Ultra-violet rays, variation of.. 18
Urticaria 197

Vitiligo 198

Water drinking 102
Wet sheet rub 146
White clothing 26
Winternitz 10
  observations of 59
Women, diseases of........... 204
Wounds, light treatment of.... 190

CPSIA information can be obtained
at www.ICGtesting.com
Printed in the USA
BVOW09s1633101116

467348BV00001B/9/P